uccess Through Effective Entrepreneurship

Alan D. Burton

TABLE OF CONTENTS

LIST OF TABLES

LIST OF FIGURES

ABSTRACT

This study is important for individuals to investigate the actions that entrepreneurs take to facilitate successful business results that meet its goals and objectives. This research identifies the importance of leadership skills on the effectiveness of business and society overall. The purpose of this study is to describe the actions effective leaders take to articulate a successful vision, establish an industry through financial support, understand different cultures, deal with global industries, and make employees more efficient. The research questions addressed in this study are focused on issues that entrepreneurs face while building an organization and the implications of the actions and decisions of leaders in entrepreneurial companies. Data were gathered through interviews with successful entrepreneurial leaders. The outcome of the study showed that there were several ways to build and improve a business and help entrepreneurs to obtain financial support through many resources.

Chapter 1: Overview

Introduction

Entrepreneurs who have a clear vision and solid financial plan tend to create successful enterprise operations that contribute to the economic well-being and competitiveness of the nation as well as contributing to the quality of life for both the organization's employees and the customers whom they serve.

Entrepreneurs face many risks when launching a business, such as economic risks, political risks, and social risks. However, they should create an attractive environment to help the economy become better by creating new jobs. Once entrepreneurs bring goods and services to the market successfully, the community often characterizes entrepreneurs as authentic leaders. During the economic crisis and difficult times when business policies are frequently changing, entrepreneurs should seek advice and guidance from reliable leaders (Jensen & Luthans, 2006).

The performance of an entrepreneur can be examined through their educational background, previous work experience, or occupational skills. These performance measures have important advantages for the workplace to build and make sound decisions (Harada, 2003). There are fundamental qualities for an entrepreneur such as leadership, management ability, and team building (Reich, 2002).

There are many definitions about entrepreneurs and how they differ from each other. According to Cantillon (1931), an entrepreneur is someone who possesses a project or scheme and assumes the major responsibility for the inherent risk and the potential rewards. Entrepreneurs are ambitious leaders who create a new environment with their employees and their corporate capital to produce new goods and services in the market. Entrepreneurs also have a fiduciary responsibility to preserve and grow the equity capacity of their organization. Similarly, Hisrich, Peters, and Shepherd (2005), define entrepreneurship as a procedure of generating something new and significant by dedicating the essential time and effort, including intuition, financial support, and social risks which will lead to prosperous results.

The current study is designed to establish a foundation of general entrepreneurial practices which are essential in creating, developing, and executing a successful venture. It is highly important to consider what kinds of financing would be most beneficial to sustain the growth and viability of business ventures. Entrepreneurs assume significant responsibility for the inherent risks and outcomes of their businesses. They can create entirely new industries with their creativity, vision, and intelligence. This study will also show what a successful leader would do to combine capital, land, and labor when starting a new business. In addition, dealing with global industries and understanding different cultures are also important factors in the growth of businesses.

Background

During a bad economy, new emerging and innovative small companies providing better and cheaper consumer products and services can place pressure on experienced entrepreneurs and corporations. Investors, however, need to see potential for return in order to justify the risk of loss. Also, entrepreneurs must have a solid business plan that is supported by their balance sheet and a viable business plan.

This study is designed to identify obstacles and benefits for building a start-up business and the outcomes experienced by entrepreneurs. The outcomes of this study are expected to demonstrate that entrepreneurs frequently have a different vision for establishing and maintaining their enterprise. Entrepreneurs can benefit from the guidance they receive from consultants and experienced leaders to solve conflicts that might be problematic at their workplace. Resolving conflicts and the ability to work with a diverse group of employees is an important entrepreneurial skill. The failure to demonstrate such organizational and personal skills can often damage relationships and ultimately impact the effectiveness of the business.

Problem Statement

In today's economy, growing businesses can be a risky challenge. It is noticeable that the economy headed into collapse in 2007, but now it is improving substantially. In fact, the economy was increasing powerfully before 2008. During the crisis, some organizations closed their businesses reflecting worry in the community to find alternatives consumer products or services (O'Connell, 2005). Effective entrepreneurs use strategic planning to solve their fundamental problems, such as finding financial support, when the economy goes down. Moreover, strategic planners face several concerns about global industries in which the company must operate. Business organizations and effective entrepreneurs should be able to raise capital based upon market demands for the services and products they offer. Then, the stability would help make "price movements, interest rates, and market growth more predictable" (p. 47). Some companies obtain financial support through dealing with international firms. When industries corporate and conceptualize the uncertainly problems with each other, then managerial departments take action to solve issues. There are significant categories to increase companies' efficiency, such as establishing administrative responsibility location, a high level of vision, and strategic orientation to facilitate people to provide the products and services (Klein, 1984). The major issues facing entrepreneurial and their organization include the following:

1. Some entrepreneurs have limited ways to receive financial supports.

2. Many leaders are not aware of foreign policies when it comes to operating and collaborating a business overseas.

3. Some entrepreneurs do not understand different organizational cultures and how to navigate social, political, economic and cultural differences.

4. Some entrepreneurs lack the leadership qualities that are required to improve their business and develop a superior work team.

Purpose Statement

The purpose of this study is to identify effective leadership skills that enable the entrepreneur to create a successful vision, secure appropriate financial support, understand diverse cultures, deal with global industries, and make employees more efficient. It is important to learn the steps that can be taken to enable successful businesses to meet their goals and objectives. Through this study, the researcher will identify the importance of leadership skills and how global leaders can work successfully in diverse cultures. Entrepreneurs bring growth to the market and new products and services through the visions they develop. They can bring economies of scale to make business a more dynamic playing field.

Furthermore, it is necessary to examine the differences between novice and experienced entrepreneurs in order to analyze their work accomplishments. These differences include entrepreneurs' leadership, attitude, confidence, innovation, and work efficiency. This study will also discuss the growth in entrepreneurship when a government protects entrepreneurs from risks or bad economic times. It will demonstrate the steps that a person should take when becoming an entrepreneur and a successful leader. Lastly, this study guides the opportunity to novice and experienced entrepreneurs to learn about manners and business atmosphere.

Research Questions

The main research question is:

1. What are the essential core practices, strategies, and qualities that foster entrepreneurial success?

Other subsequent research questions include the following:

2. What are the most important successful entrepreneurial qualities to embrace in a highly competitive world market?
3. What factors are likely to result in a successful business?
4. What core traits are essential to emphasize in a cyclical or uncertain market?
5. What kind of person makes a successful entrepreneur?

Significance of Topic

The importance of this study is to analyze the strengths and weaknesses of entrepreneurs while building and sustaining an industry. Many entrepreneurs exhibit different leadership characteristics in their workplace and entire life. These leadership qualities might be effective or ineffective depending on the entrepreneur. Therefore, the findings of this study may provide a clear image of entrepreneurs' qualities and may help leaders take effective action to establish successful ventures. In addition, this study will explore many ways to help receive capital through investors and governmental loans. Many entrepreneurs are uncertain about how to find ways to raise their capital. Who entrepreneurs go to depends on the possibility of receiving financial support at an attractive valuation. Novice and experienced entrepreneurs must create a plan to raise the funds for future business requirements.

Currently, in the 2014 business world, many entrepreneurs depend on private investors in order to seed funding before venture capitalists will provide additional financial support. It is necessary to think through the help an organization receives, and choose the backers at an early stage, to create a successful business. In addition, an important factor is to start an industry with investors who have great reputations, which results in an increase in funding from venture capitalists. In order to get a venture capitalist involved, entrepreneurs must prove the benefits of technology and increase effort to convince customers about their product concept and receive positive feedback (Chang, 1999). In order to receive funds from people, entrepreneurs must have a high level of confidence in their organization goals. In addition, lacking a supportive board will result in unpleasant consequences for entrepreneurs' business. It is important to discuss the economic conditions that might effect the business overall. Entrepreneurs are cautious at making decisions in order to prevent possible damage to their organization.

Further, this study is important for individuals who are planning to cooperate and launch a business globally. It is important to learn about foreign policies and laws when operating a business overseas, because a country's policy can harm someone's business if he or she did not obey an unfamiliar law. This study will investigate how entrepreneurs successfully established a business overseas and created positive business outcome.

Key Assumptions

There are several key assumptions for this study. First, the selected participants are very diverse which includes successful local and international entrepreneurs. Their business are commonly found in NASDAQ specializing in electronic devices, consulting services, educational programs, online services, and legal advice. This will benefit start-up business individuals to gain new ideas from various entrepreneurs to establish successful ventures. Additionally, it will help entrepreneurs to cooperate with local and global organizations efficiently. This will save time and money to ensure that individuals are aware of foreign policies, understand the different cultures, and the needs to establish a firm or cooperation overseas. Experienced entrepreneurs will learn new effective methods from international entrepreneurs to maintain a successful organization. Many organizations globally hire diverse employees purposely in order to come up with new business concepts that help to improve entrepreneurs' businesses.

Next, the selected participants are novice and experienced entrepreneurs, which would clarify many aspects in the entrepreneurial endeavor. The samples will identify the greatest failures, as a novice entrepreneur, before they met with their current success and the outcomes by experienced entrepreneurs to maintain successful organization. All participants contributed to assessments and short surveys to examine their leadership skills, financial support, and knowledge about local and international regulations.

Key Definitions

The following key terms used in this study are defined and designated below:

- Participants: Entrepreneurs interviewed for the study.
- Personal values: The quality, behavior, and personal beliefs of entrepreneurs.
- Diversity: Local and international entrepreneurs who have different work experience, educational background, culture, religion, and language

- Insights: A deep insight of complex situation. Seizing the inner and outer nature.

- Size: The participant size will be limited to 15 entrepreneurs.

- Experience: Entrepreneurs will be selected from organizations that made successful assets. The collection of knowledge and skills resulting from entrepreneurs.

- Behavior: How entrepreneurs respond to a complex situation.

- Type of participants: Entrepreneurs with solid background and skills in finance, law, technology, education, and online services.

- Social life: Attending entrepreneurship clubs, undertaking voluntary services, and participating in philanthropy.

- Self-awareness: Being fully confidant, honest, and motivated.

- Capital: How entrepreneurs target investors, receive financial supports, and sustain their business during bad economic times.

- Location: How entrepreneurs determine the best and appropriate location to start their business and stay away from their competitors.

- Credibility: Building trusts among employees and create work achievement in the workplace.

- Competition: How entrepreneurs avoid competitive lead times.

- Consulting: How entrepreneurs seek successful consultants to improve their business and what were most flaws of entrepreneurs' organization.

- International business relations: The outcomes of cooperating with international organizations, which most commonly results in monetary profits and outstanding reputation.

- Characteristics: Do entrepreneurs have the necessary diplomacy skills? Are they adept at making decisions?

- Innovation: Keeping up with today's technology and encourage employees to come up with new business ideas.

- Trait: Quality and skills of entrepreneurs

- Cost efficiency: Savvy with financial and market analysts.

- Ethics: Demonstrate superior work environment by showing sympathy, equality, and humbleness.

- Communication: How effective communication can change behaviors and convince personal opinion.

- Accountability: The ability to take someone's responsibility.

- Conversant: How entrepreneurs are knowledgeable with local and foreign policies?

Limitation of the Study

This research will be limited to founders of organizations that have a hundred employees or fewer. This research will be restricted by the methods chosen to collect data from entrepreneurs concerning their business results and leadership traits. In addition, the usual limitation of face-to-face and telephone interviews will be conducted. Some could argue that the selected participants may not provide a range of perspectives across different industries. However, it will be essential to interview various entrepreneurs who have different visions of their business's future in order to gain multi ideas maintain a successful organization.

Summary

The main purpose of entrepreneurship is the freedom from regulations, policies, and commands (Timmons, 1978). This study will also examine the differences between novice and experienced entrepreneurs in order to analyze their work accomplishments and leadership skills. Novice and experienced entrepreneurs who accomplished their vision and established a steadfast organization have reached life satisfaction. Effective entrepreneurs focus on how to improve productivity, and increase productivity among employees in order to grow a small business into a larger one. Also, entrepreneurship skill has the potential capability to translate knowledge into action, which leads to a superior performance (Schermerhorn, Osborn, & Hunt, 2003).

This research will analyze the final outcomes of interviewing entrepreneurs in terms of business results. This will include outcomes that are determined to be good for the organizations, good for the entrepreneurs, or good for the bottom line. Additionally, this study will illustrate major problems for entrepreneurs to stay in business such as lack of financial support, inability to understand foreign policies, intercultural disagreement, and competitive times during a bad economy. However, theories and critical models will be provided to understand and solve major issues. The outcomes will facilitate entrepreneurs to overcome their barriers and articulate a successful organization.

Chapter 2: Literature Review

Overview

The literature review is organized into the history of entrepreneurship, discussion of theoretical framework, research questions background, and vital fundamental of entrepreneurs' leadership skills. The purpose of this chapter is to review the current research literature of the entrepreneurs' success through core leadership skills.

Historical Background

The term entrepreneur was defined as a person who undertakes an enterprise. During the 16th century, businesses were a common term and a person who is responsible for undertaking a business venture was often called an entrepreneur (Cantillon, 1931). In the 18th century, Richard Cantillon added that an entrepreneur tolerates risk as part of his work diligence:

These definitions vary from an entrepreneur being responsible for employing resources in high productivity areas to earn profits, to risk bearing, and finally to an entrepreneur being responsible for organization and control. However, the most substantial research into entrepreneurial theory was achieved in the 20th century, under the aegis of Joseph Schumpeter, who claims that the entrepreneur has a creative destruction innovation by replacing destroying an existing economy by a better advance one. (Landes, Mokyr, & Baumol, 2012, p. 44)

According to Hebert and Link (2009), Richard Cantillion was the first writer to recognize the role of entrepreneurship and he provided a summary of his view of entrepreneurship. Cantillion described an entrepreneur as someone who involves in exchange for profits and studies business judgment in the face of uncertainty. This uncertainty involves future sales that an entrepreneur buys at a certain value to sell again at uncertain price, with considering the risks and circumstances that this sales might be profitable or loss. Jones and Wadhwani (2006) demonstrated that

> Business historians have made significant contributions to the study of entrepreneurship through their diverse coverage of countries, regions and industries, and in contrast to much management research over the past two decades through exploring how the economic, social, organizational, and institutional context matters to evaluating entrepreneurship. (p. 2)

In the beginning of the 20th century, a few historians and ancient psychologists had moved beyond the institutional angle by revamping the behavior and thinking entrepreneurs use to create success. German ancient sociologists discovered the role of religion and social interactions in the growth of modern entrepreneurial attitude toward economic improvement and economic opportunity.

Theoretical Framework

According to the Lucky and Minai (2011) theoretical framework of entrepreneurs, there are three key variables: "self-management, personal effectiveness, and performance" (p. 23) that are used to help a businessperson to become a more prosperous and successful entrepreneur. This theoretical framework suggests that self-management affects the overall of an entrepreneur's personal effectiveness and performance as well as personal effectiveness in turn affects performance. Figure 1 indicates the theoretical framework "proposes direct relationship between self-management and personal effectiveness and between self-management and performance.

However, the relationship between self-management and personal effectiveness will also affect performance" (Lucky & Minai, 2011, p. 25).

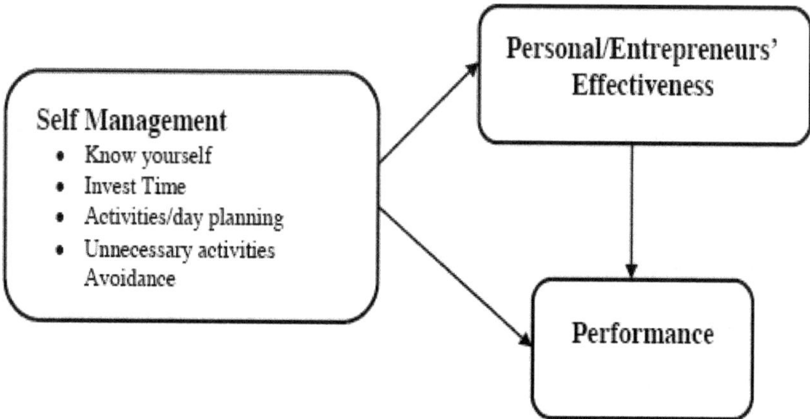

Figure 1. The Lucky and Minai theoretical framework. Adapted from "The conceptual framework of entrepreneurs and self-management," by E. A. Lucky and M. Minai, 2011, *International Journal of Business and Social Science*, 21, p. 2. Copyright 2003 by the American Psychological Association.

Lucky and Minai (2011) demonstrated that some entrepreneurs continue to be unproductive as a result of their failure to lead themselves, which is essential for the entrepreneurs' personal achievement and company performance. Self-management demands crucial and thoughtful attention in entrepreneurial discourse and should not be ignored.

Othman (2010) has a similar framework, which posits the importance of self-management that helped entrepreneurs to successfully plan, organize, coordinate, and control their industry and entrepreneurial actions. He indicated that effective self-management would lead to personal success and in turn transform into successful business performance. Correspondingly, Bennett (2007) noted that self-management helps entrepreneurs to lessen occupational and personal pressure and keep them interested in their industrial and entrepreneurial activities. Therefore, it is theorized that entrepreneurs and managers who consider and emphasize self-management has high possibility to accomplish business success.

Establishing a Foundation for Successful Entrepreneurship

In this section, the study identifies imperative entrepreneurial skills that lead to a successful business and maintain prosperous results. A successful entrepreneur certainly would apply leadership priorities in the workplace in order to create a thriving business. Many entrepreneurs pose different leadership skills in their workplace. This study provides a wide range of fundamental leadership traits to maintain major aspects of cooperating and collaborating with industries, obtaining financial supports, insuring competitive times, dealing with employees and customers, and seeking a flawless consultant to improve the weaknesses of an entrepreneur's business.

Leadership Behavior

Leaders who have effective behaviors are respected by their followers. Examining leader's behavior is one of the best ways to analyze and understand their character. Initiation of structure and consideration behaviors is one of the most commonly used models for understanding the impact of leader behavior in research (Yukl, 2006). Leaders who are sociable, open minded, loyal, encouraging, and consultative are considered to be successful (Burns, 2005).

Effective leaders focus on how to improve productivity, and increase satisfaction among employees in order to grow a small business into a larger one (Strang, 2004). Leadership skills have the potential capability to translate knowledge into action, which leads to a preferred performance (Schermerhorn, Osborn, & Hunt, 2003). According to George, Mclean, and Craig

(2008) one leadership source states, "by examining your life story and your crucible, you can understand your passions and discover the purpose of your leadership" (p. 130). Furthermore, a leader who has emotional maturity has the necessary leadership skills to optimize his skills and talents as a leader. Emotional maturity allows the leader to build strong relationships and positive interactions with other. Emotional maturity has four categories of behaviors which include: accurately identifying one's own and other's emotions, using one's own emotions to make a positive impact on others, understanding the emotions of others, and managing one's own emotional reactions (Goleman, 1998, 2000).

According to Kotter (1998), it is essential to lead and manage effectively in order to achieve stability between management and leadership. It may be assumed that not everyone is able to direct and manage efficiently. Additionally, companies are expected to employ and develop executives with mutual leadership competencies. According to Mathers (2006), it is a responsibility of managers to review the performance of employees on a consistent basis, because a lack of engagement will cost the company money and time in the long run.

Corporate Culture / International Culture

Every culture has its own style of behavior and it is clearly different from one country to another. Therefore, it is necessary for international leaders to understand the importance of leadership behavior in diverse culture (Connerley & Pedersen, 2005; House, Hanges, & Javidan, 2004). It is apparent that culture interventions through business have moral and immoral corporate which results in different consequences such as disagreement in an organization environment (Peters, 1988). In order to make successful corporate culture, leaders have to share values and behavior norms. Shared values might be effective or ineffective that most people in a group share in common. Effective values have several advantages for the company such that, "anyone who has worked in special education for more than a few years has witnessed the reappearance of numerous suspect ideas often asserting great influence in the industry and without the benefit of replicated research" (Zigler & Hall, 1986, p. 242). On the other hand, "the appearance and initial use of ineffective interventions is not necessarily inappropriate, as long as once they are deemed inappropriate or ineffective they are modified until their effectiveness is demonstrably increased or remain deliberately unselected" (Bailey, 1992, p. 139). Moreover, "the appearance and use of ineffective interventions damages the credibility of professionals who use them and unquestioningly accept them as gospel, especially when such blind acceptance is directly opposed to available empirical evidence" (Bailey, 1992, p. 59). Shared values are invisible in that leaders have to infer them based on what people do and what they emphasize when they are talking. In contrast, behavior norms are agreed upon ways of behaving in an organization and evolve over time. Rarely are behavioral norms directly discussed and agreed upon. The norms are self-sustaining, because people act in ways to support them whether they realize it or not (Kavale & Forness, 1983, 1987; Kavale & Mattson, 1983).

The purpose of enhancing corporate culture is to serve customer needs, workers, stockholders, and the society (Kotter, 1994). Successful leaders design their entire industry system around customer loyalty. When leaders build connection with the society, then they will serve customers' needs in a better environment. In addition, it is necessary for an organization to deliver superior value and attains customer loyalty, because market shares and revenues increase the company's profits. "The better economics mean the company can pay workers better, which sets off a whole chain of events. Increased pay boosts employee morale and commitment as employees stay longer" (Reichheld, 1993, p. 91).

Communication / Strategic Alliances

Building relationships between organizations can result in a greater reputation and expanded market share (Schermerhorn et al., 2003). According to Inkpen (2003), "Joint ventures and strategic alliances are commonplace in business. Strategic alliances between businesses are collaborative organizational arrangements that use resources and/or governance structures from more than one existing organization" (p. 79). The reasons for these associations consist of various driving forces such as mutual advantages, partnership, and development through joint evaluation (Inkpen, 2003). Communicators allow their managers to articulate the industry's progresses and fortes to exterior audiences (Reynolds, 2003).

Understanding the personality of other leaders' communication is very useful in creating effective relationships with others. According to Jung (1971), individuals can be categorize by two dimensions, each represent by two opposite:

- Sensing vs. Intuition (S-N)
- Thinking vs. Feeling (T-F)

This creates four possible personality groups, each have distinct communication character, marked as **ST**, **NT**, **SF** and **NF**. The following figure by Jung (1971) determines the communication characteristics of whether the other individual is a sensing (S) or an intuitive (I) type, or whether the individual is thinking (T) or feeling (F) type:

<table>
<tr><td colspan="2">S (Sensing)</td></tr>
<tr><td>

- Practical
- Relies on facts, numbers; specific
- Present-oriented, concerned about problem in hand

</td><td>

VS.

</td></tr>
</table>

<table>
<tr><td>N (iNtuition)</td></tr>
<tr><td>

- Insightful and inspirational
- Relies on insights, theories, trends of development
- Future-oriented

</td></tr>
</table>

<table>
<tr><td colspan="2">T (Thinking)</td></tr>
<tr><td>

- Governed by a rational beginning, reason
- Objective, cold and impersonal
- Uses logical analysis and objective methodologies to solve problems and make decisions

</td><td>

VS.

</td></tr>
</table>

<table>
<tr><td>F (Feeling)</td></tr>
<tr><td>

- Governed by emotional beginning, feelings
- Shows sympathy, warmth, concern and support to others
- Makes decisions and solves problems based on "gut feeling", values, "good"/"bad", "like"/"dislike"

</td></tr>
</table>

Figure 2. Sensing vs. intuitive and thinking vs. feeling. Reprinted from *Psychological types* (p. 44), by C. G. Jung, 1971, Princeton, NJ: Princeton University Press. Copyright 2007 by First Princeton.

A combination of S-N and T-F determines the personality of communicators type group, which he/she would belong to either: **ST, NT, SF** or **NF**. The table below by Jung (1971) précised what communication type would be applicable when communicating to many personality styles.

Table 1.

Communication Styles and Personality

With ST people	**With NT people**
• Be specific, confident, well-reasoned • Demonstrate immediate advantages, profit • Provide examples; use visual aids	• Be specific, well-reasoned; use visual aids, diagrams • Use concepts, theories • Appeal to intellectual capabilities • Give them a challenge • Show how the problem in hand or subject of communication fits into the big picture.
With SF people	**With NF people**
• Be supportive, expressive, and confident • Provide examples; demonstrate immediate advantages, profit • Appeal to feelings and emotions	• Be expressive, well-reasoned • Use visual aids • Use concepts, theories • Appeal to their intuition • Give them a challenge • Show how the problem in hand or subject of communication fits into the big picture

Note. Adapted from *Psychological types* (p. 64), by C. G. Jung, 1971, Princeton, NJ: Princeton University Press. Copyright 2007 by First Princeton.

Leader Skills

Mintzberg (1983) argued that in order to be successful in political arenas, leaders need to possess political skills. Therefore, rivalry with demands and complex atmosphere will make businesses increasingly more political. Luthans (2002), questioned "how does the successful leader know what behaviors are appropriate given a particular situation? Leader performance and career success are determined less by intelligence and more by social astuteness and savvy" (p. 132).

Goleman (1995) defines the soft skills as emotional intelligence. The possession and use of soft skills contributes more to an individual's ultimate achievement or failure than technical abilities or astuteness. According to Zornada (2005), "Good leaders were found to have [an] extremely strong sense of self awareness and adapted their behaviors accordingly. They have a strong sense of what they were good at and, more importantly, what they were not good at" (p. 62).

Furthermore, combining the skill with capability to exert control in community situations would cultivate one's social network and social assets. It is seen as a serious proficiency in recent attempts to model leadership as a political fact (Ammeter, Douglas, Gardner, Hochwarter, & Ferris, 2002). Interpersonal perceptiveness and the ability to adjust one's performance are important factors for social skills to change difficult situations and control the responses of workforce (Ferris, 2001).

The research categorized leader capabilities into such areas as technical skills, conservational skills, logical skills, interpersonal skills, theoretical skills, and social traits (Galpin & McEwen, 1987; Green, 1981; Priest, 1985, 1987; Riggins, 1985; Swiderski, 1981). Additionally, researchers found out that there are two significant ways of skill achievement. First, structure of skill acquisition as employees performs duties (Ackerman, 1987; Fleishman, 1972). Second, the procedures involved as individuals obtain facts and skills in different fields of experience (Anderson, 1993).

Financial Capital

Many people who are planning to initiate a business are uncertain about how to find ways to raise their capital. Therefore, they need to establish technical decisions, avoid difficult competitive situations, and obtain market data to test their business plan. Whom leaders go to depends on the possibility of receiving financial support at an attractive valuation, entrepreneurs must create a plan to raise the funds for future business requirements. Today in the business world, many people depend on private investors in order to seed funding before venture capitalists will provide additional financial support. It is necessary to recognize the help an organization receives, and choose the backers at an early stage, to create a successful business. In addition, it is important factor to start an industry with investors who have great reputations, which result in rising funding from venture capitalists. One of the methods to get a venture capitalist involved, entrepreneurs must prove the technology and make a lot of effort to convince customers about their product concept and receive positive feedback. In order to receive funds from people, they must have a high level of confidence in entrepreneurs' industry model. Because entrepreneurs want to make sure that the amount of financial support is sufficient to reach their goals and objectives. Lacking a supportive board will result in unpleasant consequences for a start-up business (Chang, 1999).

Novice & Experienced Entrepreneurs

It is necessary to examine the differences between novice and experienced entrepreneurs in order to analyze their work accomplishments in leadership, attitude, confidence, innovation and work efficiency. The researcher Hooks (2010) was concerned about the growth in entrepreneurship such as; can a government protect entrepreneurs from risks or bad economic times? How did persons become entrepreneurs? Who is a successful leader? Do manners and atmosphere determine entrepreneurship? Are there differences between female and male entrepreneurs?

According to Hooks (2010), novice and experienced entrepreneurs accomplished their life fulfillment and the new entrepreneurs looked like the happiest. This could probably be due to the innovation of business endeavor, the independence to express new trends, and generally the reality of owning an industry. In addition, new entrepreneurs presented lower perceived confidence than experienced entrepreneurs; this implied that new entrepreneurs need more development in this aspect or might not have had enough responsibility for the long-term improvement of their business. Schumpeter (1939) believed that entrepreneurs want to overcome barriers, enjoy creating, and like to exercise their creativity.

Kemelgor (1985) explained that some of the major reasons for failures of several entrepreneurs actions within the first three years included "financial problems, lack of effective marketing or promotion, and lack of management skills" (p. 44). Kemelgor (1985) suggested that to make more effort for the need of entrepreneurs to be well trained in superior administration practices in order to avoid the risks that affect various entrepreneurial activities within the first three years.

Entrepreneurship is a fundamental factor for employment, stimulus economic development, and improvement for producing goods and services in the market. Novice entrepreneurs were happy with the decisions they made to enter into a new business and even though they were sacrificing time, effort, and personal assets, the results were worthwhile. The aspiration to be an entrepreneur was beneficial to the individual, society, and economy, if the entrepreneur became successful and financially strong (Hooks, 2010)

In order to understand how to motivate new entrepreneurs to endure in business for three or the next few years, experienced entrepreneurs concurred that one key aspect in business success was to not postpone and never put off significant matters until further time. Life satisfaction was not essentially acquired through business achievement or, how much money an entrepreneur gained. It would be wise to consider that as entrepreneurs launched, controlled and managed a business for the purpose of achievement and development, their fulfillment with life was gained (Hooks, 2010).

According to Chay (1993) and Ketz de Varies (1980), the main purpose for the self-employed is freedom from regulations, policies, and commands. Timmons (1978) identified entrepreneurial aspects as freedom to make choices, responsibility to oneself, and likely to gain successful results. Senge (2000) stated that babies were born with innovative characteristics. They wanted to discover, identify to see how things work, and to examine how to create their environments into success.

Decision Making

Decision-making is a process of first defining a problem, then looking at alternatives to solve that problem, then determining the best choice and implementing that solution. Strong decision-making is a crucial character trait differentiating high performers from the vast levels of the mediocre. The most effective individuals make decisions swiftly and change them slowly. In contrast, unsuccessful people are very slow to make decisions, perhaps choosing not to make one (which is, in itself, a decision) and they change decisions they have made very rapidly (Tracy, 2009).

Entrepreneurs must be adept at making decisions in any difficult situation, therefore, certain key steps are necessary for entrepreneurs to modify the situation. These steps include: define, understand, identify, evaluate, review, and take action. However, making decisions fairly quickly does not mean that decisions are made intuitively or without information. Usually there is some kind of definitive process involved but different processes suit different situations (Tracy, 2009).

Decision-making is imperative in most organizations, which would lead to successful outcomes. The following figure by Akrani (2011), explains the benefits of decision making in an organization.

Figure 3. Importance of decision-making. Reprinted from *Importance of Decision Making in Management,* by G. N. Akrani, 2011, Retrieved from http://kalyan-city.blogspot.com/2011/08/ importance-of-decision-making-in.html. Copyright 2006 by Kalyan City Life.

Most successful companies have a set of values and beliefs, which guide them in making decisions. While every company has a different focus, these values may very simply. For example, will this change be good for the community? Or, will this change be harmful to the environment? If the proposed change does not fit with the guiding principles of the company it should not be implemented regardless of the internal benefits.

Development Program for Employees

Every department and business has its own environment. The work atmosphere changes in any department or organization when one manager replaces another. In a matter of days, the environment can be dissimilar when the manager leaves; there will be no climate then employees would create their own of environment that is completely different.

High levels of teamwork and collaboration would produce high levels of efficiency, confidence, faithfulness, and job satisfaction. When staffs see that they are creative and meeting or achieving objectives, then they tend to intellect-improved levels of personal accomplishment, self-assurance and self-esteem. Many managers emphasize the magnitude of teamwork, but almost all of the rewards and gratitude they provide are based on person performance. If entrepreneurs truthfully want to build teamwork in the department, they need to reward it (Lloyd, 2002).

A successful work team is a small number of individuals with matching abilities who are dedicated to a mutual purpose, set of performance objectives, and approach for which they hold themselves equally responsible. By facilitating teamwork in the workplace, it will result in generating respectful performances, developing communication, becoming better able to execute work responsibilities together, and building strong relationships. The demand for project management (PM) training is increasing as more organizations use project team methods. Also, most employees have little exposure to training in the field. Project managers would develop employees' knowledge and learning which helps improve project performance.

In addition, it is necessary to set goals for employees which are simple and effective in the workplace. Supervisors need to devote attention to employee goal setting to create higher levels of efficiency among group members. After setting worker goals in the workplace, entrepreneurs can determine the objective by looking at different aspects such as; cost, quality, quantity, or timeliness. Delivering feedback is central to keeping people inspired and knowing how they are succeeding towards the objective (Deines, 2006). The following figure explains the importance of decision making among team members.

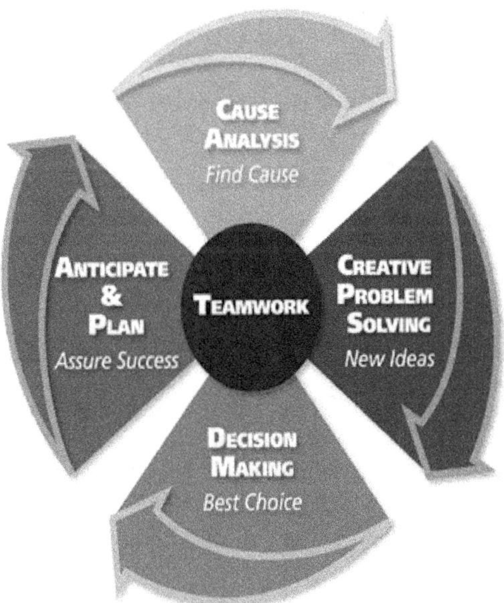

Figure 4. Problem solving & decision-making. Reprinted from *Action Management Associates*, by S. B. Smith, 2012, Retrieved from http://actionm.com.

Superior Management

Each company has its own leader to represent their management team. Those leaders might be effective or ineffective leaders. A successful entrepreneur is a person who can manage a business successfully, has great communication skills, handles issues well, and is knowledgeable about managing people in their social and business functions. In general, powerful leaders can lead a business into major success, which can lead to dramatic outcomes.

An entrepreneur must always be ten steps ahead of their competition. Being ten steps ahead of their competition allows them to be much more successful enterprise. Also, entrepreneurs must have dedicated staff members who share the same goals about the company's mission. Having a dedicated staff will lead to a brighter company by sharing ideas back and forth which will promote a better efficiency leading to cost cutting and ultimately profitability.

Time management is an important role to make manager's attitude effective and productive. Entrepreneurs must be specific in their characteristic such as measurable, achievable, realistic, time, and not vague (Forsyth, 2007).

Leadership Challenges

Entrepreneurs must always note trends in consumer's behavior. It is vital to have a consumer relationship management team who is dedicated to following trends in consumer behaviors and make sure that entrepreneur providing superior features and benefits over the competition.

Kouzes (2007) states that the leadership challenge is about how leaders mobilize others to desire to acquire astonishing results in firms. It is about the practices that leaders use to change "values into actions, visions into realities, obstacles into innovations, separateness into solidarity, and risks into rewards" (p. 33). It is about leadership that creates the environment in which people turn challenging opportunities into significant successes.

Leadership as one of the three factors required for a new business creation including team collaboration, building trust, and being a self-starter (Timmons & Spinelli, 2004). Additionally, Gibb (1993) demonstrated behaviors as innovative that created to persuade others using capabilities and traits such as "persuasiveness, negotiations, planning, and decision taking" (p. 77). These traits and skills are parts of what leadership possess.

According to Colin (2004), some people were born with entrepreneurial characteristics and will achieve in their businesses with or without education, even though no amount of institutions can guarantee business achievement for those who do not have the entrepreneurial spirit. Katz (1992) indicated that the most significant aspects for entrepreneurs are independence, talent, capital, innovation, and integration. Kouzes and Posner (2002) listed five exemplary leadership practices as:

1. Modeling the way.

2. Inspiring a shared vision.

3. Challenging the process.

4. Enabling others to act.

5. Encouraging the heart.

The following figure by Kouzes and Posner (2002), explains the five practices of

leadership challenge that every entrepreneur should learn to improve the overall of his/her

business:

The Five Practices of Exemplary Leadership®	Ten Commitments
Model the Way	• **Clarify values by finding your voice** and affirming shared ideals. • **Set the example** by aligning actions with shared values.
Inspire a Shared Vision	• **Envision the future** by imagining exciting and ennobling possibilities. • **Enlist others** in a common vision by appealing to shared aspirations.
Challenge the Process	• **Search for opportunities** by seizing the initiative and by looking outward for innovative ways to improve. • **Experiment and take risks** by constantly generating small wins and learning from experience.
Enable Others to Act	• **Foster collaboration** by building trust and facilitating relationships. • **Strengthen others** by increasing self determination and developing competence.
Encourage the Heart	• **Recognize contributions** by showing appreciation for individual excellence. • **Celebrate the values and victories** by creating a spirit of community.

Figure 5. The five practices of leadership challenge. Reprinted from *The Leadership Challenge*

(p. 158), by J. M. Kouzes and B. Z. Posner, 2002, San Francisco, CA: Jossey-Bass. Copyright

2000 by John Wiley & Sons.

This model helps a leader to provide superior leadership in times where context of management are challenged by events such as new economy or competition. An entrepreneur is responsible to create an environment where employees turn challenging opportunities into remarkable success.

Entrepreneurial Parents

Parents played a significant role in an inclination toward entrepreneurship. Hooks (2010) explained:

Parents who owned their own business could be a source of great inspiration to a young child. Research also found that education was important in the upbringing of an entrepreneur. There were many examples of people who left school or university without completing their studies and who became successful entrepreneurs. However, education does play a role in how entrepreneurs handle problems and their ability to manage their business. (p. 45)

Diplomacy in Entrepreneurialism

Diplomacy is the ability to facilitate debates between accredited people representing members or nations. It frequently refers to global relationships, dealing with international diplomacy through the arbitration of professional diplomats with regard to matters of trade (Ernest, 1998).

According to Karimi (2006), diplomacy is the proficiency of dealing with attributed politicians; it is one that develops and makes key relationships and discussions in order to create agreements, consensus, or future plan. Furthermore, diplomacy is the ability of "understanding, listening, anticipating needs, and solving problems through negotiation" (p. 14). It involves a high level of identifying and specializing; it also needs the desire in order to see things from different viewpoints, and explore the environment to focus on the matter and issue as carefully as possible.

Diplomatic persons are familiar with how to approach many topics with tact and assurance; they create opportunities where they have the capabilities to overcome oppositions and barriers as they become apparent. They tend not to skip into conclusions, as the space of time between thinking and communicating is significant to the outcome of the topic. Diplomatic persons listen and speak when they need to; extreme talk or distracted attention is not a characteristic of a strong diplomat (Karimi, 2006).

Being able to 'read' persons is another skillful diplomatic function. By understanding details in a situation as character styles and communication styles of a various members, diplomatic persons can reach to productive argument, discuss, and overall solid thinking. Diplomacy does not involve in problems for the sake of accomplishing goals and objectives. Instead, diplomacy establishes relationships that have thriving results for both parties (Karimi, 2006).

Training

Employees willing to learn and receive training and improve early in their careers are expected to be more productive. Teaching and training help employees to improve their knowledge and skills. The main purpose of training is to understand the processes, perform certain procedures, enhance decision-making, and improve leadership skills (Bernatek, 2010).

The most common and economical method of training and development depends on the needs of a new worker or whether the training involves new concepts such as creating teams or introduction of new technology (Bretz & Thompsett, 1992). According to Lynch (1992), "A necessary condition for firms to gain a competitive advantage through innovative human resource utilization is that the work force is well educated, highly skilled, and broadly trained" (p. 12).

Training is based upon the need to derive efficiency and to train employees to become progressively better. Training is also to prepare new leaders to take the place of those who no longer fill leadership positions. Achievement is an aspect of business that usually requires training. Every company needs to provide training programs to encourage employees to be productive and create new ideas. The main goal of training programs is to build a team that share ideas and freedom of innovation. Team building will improve approachability, cohesiveness, and willingness to their colleagues. A working team would make increased production and quality of innovation (Lynch, 1992).

According to Gibson and Bartram (2000), training is fundamental for employees of every business. It increases the knowledge and skill of employees for completing certain tasks. It also fills the gap between the requirements of the job and the worker's ability, knowledge, and performance. Furthermore, entrepreneurs have many roles in the company. Investing in development of skills will pay the organization back. The training program is designed for new employees with little or no formal training, as well as experienced employees looking for new strategies to motivate manage and communicate. The training program would have different objectives combined to benefit employees from all aspects. The objectives of the training program are; understanding employee's roles, communicating effectively, transferring the goals, developing employee skills, accepting mistake and moving through change, and managing teams in the innovation process.

Learning

Knowles, Holton, and Swanson (2005) indicated that learning involves change and also is the acquisition of "habits, knowledge, and attitude" (p. 72). It allows people to make personal and social changes. And any change is a learning process that involves individuals with their environment, which make them able of dealing effectively (Knowles, Holton, & Swanson, 2005). Similarly, Kember and Gow (1994) defined learning as a dimensional hierarchical classification that consists of information absorbing, remembering, gaining of facts, constructing the meaning, understanding the reality, and changing as an individual.

The change from instruction to learning will not be rapid. It will be steps of gradual variation and experimentation in many organizations in order to create a new vision for the whole employees. Through the institution's assessment program, it will evaluate employee's knowledge and skills. After learning an organization's processes, employees would be acknowledged and specialized to pursue their daily missions (Robert & John, 1995).

According to Knowles et al. (2005) there are eight types of learning:

1. Signal Learning: Persons learn how to identify a task through a symbolism with signal response.

2. Stimulus-Response Learning: The learner requires a connection or instrument to a response.

3. Chaining: The acquisition of two or more stimulus responses.

4. Verbal Association: The learner use verbal to improve communicate or language.

5. Multiple Discrimination: Persons learn to make various responses according to any situation that needs to identify physical appearance.

6. Concept Learning: Individuals would be able to make similar or dissimilar responses to identify objects or events.

7. Principle Learning: Function of two or more steps that determine and control behaviors.

8. Problem Solving: Combine two or more principles to make a new capability in order to solve internal or external problems.

These eight functions represent how an individual's environment affects their ability to act with people. These conditions will make the learner able to combine principles to change behavior and performance. The teacher role is to make the learner interested, alerted, and problem oriented. Teachers must recognize and identify characteristics in the workplace that require good performance in order to produce high quality results. The materials must be clearly defined for the learner to grasp a content the first time and leave little repetition for the teacher (Knowles et al., 2005).

Teaching

Teaching is a big responsibility that any individual can carry. "The role of the teacher is often undervalued, but teaching can be rewarding and enjoyable and have lasting impacts on students" (Gordon, 2003, p. 543). There are many ways of teaching such as online teaching, in-class teaching, audio, and reading materials. Every organization must provide its employees with updates to maintain the progression of the company.

Evaluation of a Program

According to Kirkpatrick (1994), the meaning of evaluation is the "determination of the effectiveness of a training program" (p. 294). Evaluation has four logical steps as follow:

- Reaction: How did employees like the seminar?

- Learning: What standards did motivate employees to be changed?

- Behavior: How did employees change their work behavior after attending the program?

- Results: What were the benefits to an organization and employees? Increased profits? Improved working skills? Reduced cost?

The purpose of the evaluation is to inspire training people to take an in depth approach at evaluations. It teaches employees to make changes and be professional at processing many tasks that could create successful results (Kirkpatrick, 1994).

Leadership Theories

Kouzes and Posner (2002) formed a list of the features of effective entrepreneurs based on a study of more than 75,000 leaders. "The list consists following characteristics: Honest Forward-looking, Competent, Inspiring, Intelligent, Fair-minded, Broad-minded, Supportive, Straightforward, Dependable, Cooperative, Determined, Imaginative, Ambitious, Courageous, Caring, Mature, Loyal, Self-controlled and Independent" (p. 212). In addition, the following leadership theories will drive an entrepreneur's vision into a successful reality:

- Great Man Theory

- Trait Theory

- Behavioral Theory

- Emotional Intelligence Theory

- Management / Transactional Theory

- Relationship / Transformational Theory

Great Man Theory

Bass (1985) stated that the great man theory is described as born to lead. According to this standpoint, effective entrepreneurs are simply born with the fundamental personal attributes such as charisma, intelligence, political skills, and confidence that create them natural born leaders. Bass (1990) indicated the term *Great Man* was used because, at early studies of leadership often focused on male quality, especially in terms of military leadership. This theory is an example of people who were born with entrepreneurial skills such as assertiveness, social, confidence, and influential communication skills instead of acquiring them over a lifetime.

Trait Theory

This type of theory described as "people are born with inherited traits. Some traits are particularly suited to lead, making them excellent leadership qualities. People who make good leaders have the right combination of traits" (Stogdill, 1974, p. 33). Table 2 shows a list of traits and skills vital to leaders:

Table 2.

Trait Leadership Theory

Traits	Skills
•Adaptable to situations	•Clever (intelligent)
•Alert to social environment	•Conceptually skilled

(Continued)

Traits	Skills
•Ambitious and achievement-orientated	•Creative
•Assertive	•Diplomatic and tactful
•Cooperative	•Fluent in speaking
•Decisive	•Knowledgeable about group task
•Dependable	•Organized (administrative ability)
•Dominant (desire to influence others)	•Persuasive
•Energetic (high activity level)	•Socially skilled
•Persistent •Self-confident	
•Tolerant of stress	
•Willing to assume responsibility	

Note. Adapted from *Handbook of leadership* (p. 187), by R. M. Stogdill, 1974, New York, NY: Free Press. Copyright 2003 by Free Press.

This kind of theory is similar to the Great Man Theory, but in this type, the leader would make great individuals that obtain leadership qualities. The trait approach is supposed to enable individuals to behave in certain ways and build leadership characteristics. An effective entrepreneur can persuade his/her employees to change and act in a way that would make an entrepreneur's business successful.

Zaccaro (2004) created a model to explain how leader's traits influence on individuals' performance. The following figure shows that leadership occurs from the shared influence of multiple traits as apposed to developing from the independent assessment of traits. This trait model is based on leadership types of many leaders and is used to forecast leadership effectiveness.

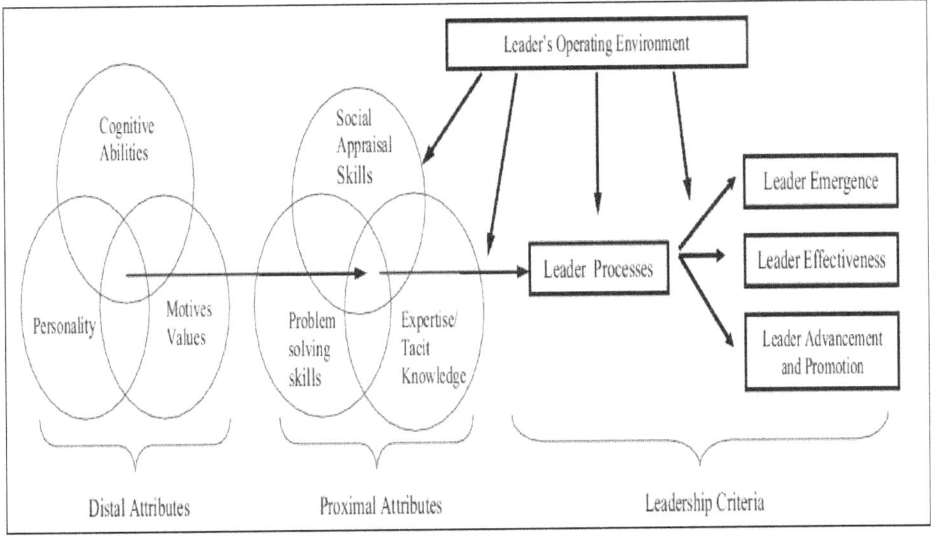

Figure 6. Leader traits. Reprinted from *The Nature of Leadership* (p. 61), by S. B. Zaccaro,

2004, Thousand Oaks, CA: Sage. Copyright 2000 by SAGE Publications.

Behavioral Theory

This kind of theory is the opposite of the Great Man Theory, which means that leaders

can be made, rather than are born. Bass (1985) indicated that the behavioral theory "focuses on

the actions of leaders not on mental qualities or internal states. People can learn to become

leaders through teaching and observation" (p. 15). In the late 1940s, Ohio State University has

conducted extensive research on this theory, and the studies categorized the behavioral

leadership theory into two types: task oriented people and people oriented leaders.

The task concerned leaders are focusing their behaviors on the organizational structure,

the operating procedures, and they likely to keep control. They will favor behaviors that

are in line with: initializing, organizing, clarifying, and information gathering. However,

the people oriented leaders are focusing their behaviors on ensuring that the inner needs of the people are satisfied. Thus, they will seek to motivate their staff through emphasizing the human relation. Leaders with a people focus will have behaviors that are in line with: inspiring, observing, listening, and training and mentoring. (Ohio State University, n.d., p 1)

The behavioral theory is imperative for entrepreneurs for two main reasons: they show concern for people and concern for production. While entrepreneurs can exhibit both kinds of behavior, typically they can consider increase in production, employee turnover, and absence declined. Moreover, entrepreneurs can empower employees to increase their performance and effectiveness. Figure 7 demonstrates a learner's perception is likely to adopt a new behavior by his or her personal attitudes, social influences, and perceived power over outcomes.

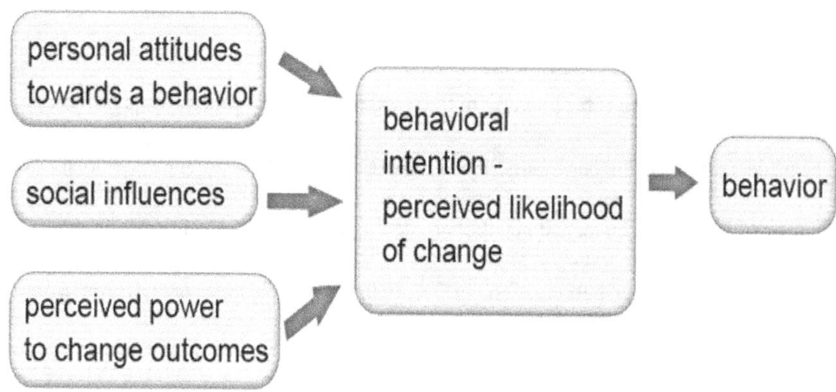

Figure 7. Theory of behavior. Reprinted from *Readiness to change and clinical success*, by K. A. Peterson, 2012, Retrieved from http://instructionaldesignfusions.com. Copyright 2011 by Instructional Design Fusions.

Emotional Intelligence Theory

The early emotional intelligence theory was originated during the 1970s and 80s and is increasingly applicable to organizational development and developing individuals. The emotional intelligence principles provide a new method to understand and examine individuals' behaviors, leadership types, attitudes, social skills, and potential. Emotional intelligence is a meaningful consideration in human resources development, job profiling, employment interviewing and selection, organizational growth, public relations, and client service (Goleman, 1995).

It is essential for entrepreneurs to use emotional intelligence in the workplace in order to produce prospering outcomes. An entrepreneur can use Goleman (1995) five emotional intelligence domains to sustain the growth of his or her business:

1. Understanding your own emotions;

2. managing your own emotions;

3. inspiring yourself;

4. identifying and understanding other individuals' emotions; and

5. managing people, for instance, dealing the emotions of others.

The following table by Lynn (2008) demonstrates different components of emotional intelligence that can be used into an organization to promote more prolific working relationships, better results, and improve personal satisfaction.

Table 3.

Components of Emotional Intelligence

Area of Emotional Intelligence	Definition	Competences
Self-Awareness and Self-Control	The ability to fully understand oneself and one's impact on others and to use that information to manage oneself productively	*Self-Awareness* • Impact on others: An accurate understanding of how one's behavior or words affect others • Emotional and inner awareness: An accurate understanding of how one's emotions and thoughts affect behaviors • Accurate self-assessment: An honest assessment of strengths and weaknesses *Self-Control* • Emotional expression: The ability to manage anger, stress, excitement, and frustration • Courage: The ability to manage fear • Resilience: The ability to manage disappointment or failure
Empathy	Ability to understand the perspective of others	• Respectful listening: Listening respectfully to others to develop a deep understanding of others' points of view • Feeling the impact on others: The ability to assess and determine how situations as well as one's words and actions affect others • Service orientation: The desire to help others

(continued)

Area of Emotional Intelligence	Definition	Competences
Social Expertness	Ability to build genuine relationships and bonds and express caring, concern, and conflict in healthy ways	• Building relationships: The ability to build social bonds • Collaboration: The ability to invite others in and value their thoughts related to ideas, projects, and work • Conflict resolution: The ability to resolve differences • Organizational savvy: The ability to understand and maneuver within organizations
Personal Influence	Ability to positively lead and inspire others as well as oneself	*Influencing Others* • Leading others: The ability to have others follow you • Creating a positive work climate: The ability to create an inspiring culture • Getting results through others: The ability to achieve goals through others *Influencing Self* Self-confidence: An appropriate belief in one's skills or abilities

(continued)

Area of Emotional Intelligence	Definition	Competences
		• Initiative and accountability: Being internally guided to take steps or actions and taking responsibility for those actions • Goal orientation: Setting goals for oneself and living and working toward goals • Optimism: Having a tendency to look at the bright side of things and to be hopeful for the best • Flexibility: The ability to adapt and bend to the needs of others or situations as appropriate
Mastery of Purpose and Vision	Ability to bring authenticity to one's life and live out one's intentions and values	• Understanding one's purpose and values: Having a clearly defined purpose and values • Taking actions toward one's purpose: Taking actions to advance one's purpose • Authenticity: Alignment and transparency of one's motives, actions, intentions, and purpose

Note. Adapted from *The EQ interview finding employees with high emotional intelligence* (p. 71), by A. N. Lynn, 2008, New York, NY: American Management Association. Copyright 2006 by AMACOM.

Management / Transactional Theory

According to Bass (1985), transactional leadership also identified as managerial leadership was originally developed in the early 1980s. It focuses on the role of management, organization, and group effectiveness. This kind of theory is based on a leadership system of rewards and punishments. Transactional theory is frequently used in business, when workers are successful, they would be rewarded; when they perform poorly, they would be punished. Northouse (2007) indicated that transactional leadership style starts with the idea that team members concur to follow their leader when they work on a project. The leader has a right to reward or punish team members based on their work to meet an appropriate standard.

Likewise, Burns (1978) indicated that with transactional leadership, employees are inspired by rewards and punishments. In addition, following the guidelines and orders of the leader is the main goal of the follower. An effective entrepreneur can consider the relationship between himself/herself and subordinates as an exchange. When employees perform well, they receive some type of reward and when they fail, they will be reprimanded. In managerial leadership theory, the essential parts include instructions, procedures, and values. Subordinates are not encouraged to be innovative or to find new keys to problems. Studies have found that managerial leadership theory tends to be most applicable in areas where problems are simple and well defined. According to Bass (1985) explained:

> Managerial leaders are extrinsic motivators. They work within existing organizational structures and shape their work according to organizational culture. These kinds of leaders use negotiation to attain their management goals, which are in sync with the organization's goals. Management by exception is part of this style, and refers to the

tendency to maintain status quo by intervening in the work of subordinates only when needed. (p. 32)

Relationship / Transformational Theory

Transformational leadership theory, also identified as relationship theory, emphases on the connections shaped among leaders and followers. Transformational leaders encourage and motivate individuals by assisting team members see the significance of the task. These leaders are dedicated to increase the performance of team members and fulfill their potential. Leaders with this type of theory often have high principals and ethical standards (Bass, 1985).

Furthermore, in any group work where someone takes control of a situation by delivering a clear vision of the group's objectives and makes the rest of the team members feel recharged and motivated, is called a transformational leader (Bass, 1985). A successful entrepreneur can motivate positive changes in those who follow. Transformational entrepreneurs are generally eager to inspire, excited to motivate, and passionate about their followers. They are also focused on ensuring the success of other group members as well.

According to Burns (1978), transformational leadership can be perceived when "leaders and followers make each other to advance to a higher level of moral and motivation." Through the talent of their vision and character, transformational leaders are able to inspire followers to alter expectations, perceptions, and inspirations to work toward common objectives. The table below by Burns shows the difference between Transactional and Transformational Leadership Theory:

Table 4.

Comparison between Transactional and Transformational Leaders

Transactional Leadership	**VS**	**Transformational Leadership**
Leadership is responsive		Leadership is proactive
Works within the organizational culture		Works to change the organizational culture by implementing new ideas
Employees achieve objectives through rewards and punishments set by leader		Employees achieve objectives through higher ideals and moral values
Motivates followers by appealing to their own self-interest		Motivates followers by encouraging them to put group interests first
Management-by-exception: maintain the status quo; stress correct actions to improve performance.		Individualized consideration: Each behavior is directed to each individual to express consideration and support. Intellectual stimulation: promote creative and innovative ideas to solve problems

Note. Adapted from *Leadership* (p. 44), by J. M. Burns, 1978, New York, NY: Harper & Row. Copyright 2000 by Management Study Guide.

Bass (1985) developed four different components of transformational leadership:

1. Intellectual Stimulation: Transformational leaders not only encounter the state of affairs; they also support creativity between followers. The leader motivates followers to discover new ways of creating things and new opportunities to learn.

2. Individualized Consideration: Transformational leadership also includes providing support and inspiration to individual followers. In order to adopt supportive relationships, transformational leaders always keep open communication so that followers may not feel uptight to share ideas.

3. Inspirational Motivation: Relationship leaders have a well-defined vision that they are capable to articulate followers. These leaders are also capable to assist followers experience the same passion and inspiration to achieve these objectives.

4. Idealized Influence: The relationship leaders perform as a role model for followers. Because followers rely and admire the leader, they imitate this individual and adopt his/her ideas.

Each of the four components explains personalities that are significant to the transformation procedure. When leaders are strong characters, models, inspires, trainers, they apply the four components to help transform their followers into better, more creative and successful people. Northouse (2001) indicates in 39 reports of transformational literature, people who showed transformational leadership were more successful leaders with better work results. According to Riggio (2009):

Transformational leaders are those who stimulate and inspire followers to both achieve extraordinary outcomes and, in the process, develop their own leadership capacity. Transformational leaders help followers grow and develop into leaders by responding to individual followers' needs by empowering them and by aligning the objectives and goals of the individual followers, the leader, the group, and the larger organization. (p. 2)

Scholars have found that this type of leadership can have a progressive influence on the group. Studies evidence clearly prove that team members led by transformational leaders have greater levels of success and satisfaction than team members led by other types of leaders. The reason is transformational leaders consider that their subordinates can do their best, leading team members to feel motivated and empowered (Riggio, 2009).

Consulting

Some entrepreneurs may lack necessary skills and/or responsibilities that are required in the workplace such as improving group's performance, increasing company's profits, training employees, designing programs, developing management, and improving organizational communications. In this case, it is highly recommended that leaders hire professional consultants to improve the overall business. An effective consultant would make a correct diagnosis by identifying needs, helping answer those needs, improving managerial performance, and achieving employee satisfaction and motivation.

According to Hom (2013), the first obligation a business consultant has is the discovery stage, where he or she aims to learn about the client's business. Effective business consultants would dedicate their time to study as much as possible about the organization from the board of directors and employees. This can involve exploring the facility, meeting with the managers and workers, evaluating the finances and reading all company's materials. Throughout this stage, the business consultant will reveal the details of an organization's mission and what procedures will be taken.

Once an in-depth understanding has been developed, a business consultant has entered the evaluation phase, where the goal is to identify where change is needed. This includes identifying the company's strengths and weaknesses, as well as current and foreseeable problems. These can include problems already seen by ownership and management, and new problems seen thanks to the business consultant's objectivity. (Hom, 2013, p. 10)

The following figure shows how a management consultant works with the clients or entrepreneurs to help improve their business.

Figure 8. The process of management consultants to work with a client.

First, the consultant would clarify goals and provide desired results of the plan. Second,

identify issues and discover the root/s of the problem/s. Third investigate, create metrics, and

collect pertinent data. Four analyze data and several value proposals. Five develop plans and key

answers to meet objectivities. Then, perform and execute on action plans and solutions. Finally, monitor and compute key metrics of implemented plans and review program performance to goals.

Additionally, Hom (2013) specified a list of reasons why entrepreneurs should consider hiring professional business consultants:

1. Provide knowledge in a specific market

2. Identify business's problems

3. Supplement the existing employees

4. Provide objectivity

5. Teach and coach workers

6. Renew an organization

7. Influence employees

8. Provide methods to grow business

9. Increase profits

10. Boost efficiency

An effective business consultant would also provide key solutions to difficulties and proposals on capitalizing on opportunities. Perhaps an organization has strong sales division but feeble marketing division; this is an opportunity for the organization to rise marketing assets and capitalize on the sales employees. During this stage, it is necessary for the consultant and the organization's teams to retain open and clear communications (Hom, 2013).

It is also significant for an entrepreneur to take the consultant's advice as positive criticism, and not as disapproval to how the entrepreneur has been doing things. The consultant transports objectivity and a fresh standpoint, where the entrepreneur is personally close to the business. The entrepreneur would indeed have feedback and provide ideas to the consultant, who should take the entrepreneur's considerations and modify plans as needed. Once the entrepreneur and the consultant concur on a plan, the consultant should enter the third stage of consulting, which is the reforming stage, or the execution of the plan. In this stage, the consultant is to construct on assets and exclude burdens, as well as observing progress on the plan and modifying as needed (Hom, 2013).

Chapter 3: Methodology

Introduction

Research is a methodical investigation to describe, explain, foresee, and control the observed phenomenon (Babbie, 1998). Research includes inductive and deductive approaches. Inductive approaches examine the observed phenomenon and classify the general values, structures, or practices underlying the phenomenon experiential. Deductive approaches validate the hypothesized values through observation. The purposes are distinctive: one is to develop descriptions, and the other is to examine the validity of the descriptions (Gall, 1996). Patton and Patton (1990), classified four imperative types of research processes that are based on different purposes:

1. Basic Research: this type of research aims to understand and explain theoretical concepts and statements that ideally generalize across time and space. This research explains the phenomenon theory under investigation to provide its contribution to knowledge.

2. Applied Research: the purpose of this research is to help individuals comprehend the nature of human problems. It provides potential solutions to individuals and social problems.

3. Evaluation Research: this type of research investigates the processes and results aimed at attempted solutions. Evaluation research consists of two types: formative and summative. The purpose of formative evaluation is to improve human intervention within definite settings such as time, place, and events. The purpose of summative evaluation is to arbitrate the effectiveness of programs, rules, or produces.

4. Action Research: this research aims to solve specific issues within a program, organization, or society. Patton and Patton (1990) explained that the design and data

gathering in action research tend to be more informal, and the individuals in the setting are involved in collecting information and learning about themselves.

This chapter describes the design of the intended research and the data collection strategies. In addition, this chapter details the quantitative approach to be used to answer the research questions and will present further details on specific samples to be surveyed, the survey instrument, and the scales utilized.

Restatement of Research Questions

The primary research question is:

1. What are the essential core practices, strategies, and qualities that foster entrepreneurial success?

The subsequent research questions are reiterated here:

2. What are the most important successful entrepreneurial qualities to embrace in a highly competitive world market?

3. What factors are likely to result in a successful business?

4. What core traits are essential to emphasize in a cyclical or uncertain market?

5. What kind of person makes a successful entrepreneur?

Selection of Research Site and Participants

The researcher selected 15 entrepreneurs from organizations that have been successful in growing the company's net worth. These entrepreneurs are the founder and CEO of their company and were invited to participate in this study. A survey approach was used to collect primary data. In addition, face-to-face and telephone interviews were conducted. Survey participants were sought from industries found through National Association of Securities Dealers Automated Quotations (NASDAQ) specializing in electronic devices, consulting services, educational programs, online services, and legal advice, among others. It is imperative to include various entrepreneurs who may have different visions and ideas of sustaining their business, which will facilitate the investigator to obtain multi ideas in order to maintain a successful business.

Protection of Human Subjects

The primary purpose of the Institutional Review Board (IRB) is to protect the human subjects, which involves participating in research activities. The Pepperdine Graduate and Professional Schools' (GPS) IRB (2009) website clearly states:

Applications submitted to the GPS IRB generally encompass social, behavioral and educational research and are usually considered medically non-invasive. The GPS IRB employs a review process in conformity with the Federal Policy for the Protection of Human Subjects and the Federal-wide Assurance (FWA) enacted between Pepperdine University and the Office for Human Research Protections (OHRP) under the Department of Health and Human Services (DHHS). ("Purpose of the GPS" para. 2)

By addressing the welfare and human subjects concerns in an applicant's anticipated study, the IRB works to guard researchers from engaging in potentially or unethical investigation practices.

The researcher took further safeguards to protect the rights and confidentiality of human participants by completing the National Institute of Health's Office of Extramural Research Web-based training course "Protecting Human Research Participants" (see Appendix A). The IRB policy states, "in the review and conduct of research, Pepperdine University is guided by the ethical principles set forth in the Belmont Report (i.e., respect the persons, beneficence, and justice)" (Graduate School of Psychology IRB Policy, 2009, p 1). The researcher filed an exempt application with the GPS IRB manager, Dr. Thema Bryant-Davis (see Appendix B). The exempt application was approved and alterations made; a copy of the IRB approval letter is enclosed in Appendix C.

The minimal risk for participants may experience is that other individuals may discover participants contributed in the study even though their identity is protected. However, all survey responses were retained confidential, so this risk is very low. Another probable minimal risk is the potential burden on the contributor's time or revealing confidential information about their organization. However, this is highly unlikely. The activities involved on this list were eligible for review through the exempt review procedure. Additionally, these activities are not extensive, thereby creating a minimal risk exposure. It should be noted that the activities listed in this study are eligible for expedited review since the conditions of this study include minimal risk to the participants.

Security of the Data

There will be no correlation between the participants' identity and data collection. In order to protect the actual data collected, the researcher will be the only person accessing the data. The data will be saved on a designated computer that belongs to the principal researcher. In addition, the data will be stored in a password-protected file and the online survey provider website will require a password to access the data. Once the survey outcomes are collected, all the data will be transferred into an external hard-drive and stored in a locked box in the researcher's home. Any information not used for the purposed of the study will be destroyed.

The pertinent data will be saved for 3 years posted the dissertation completion and the data will be terminated thus after.

In compliance with IRB, the primary researcher considered the following procedures to ensure confidentiality:

1. There were no names identified or collected of any of the contributors in the study.

2. Paper prints and all the data were stored in a safe locked box in the researcher's home.

3. Quantitative data, electronic statistical, and/or graphs were all be saved in an external hard-drive with password protected and retained in a locked box at the investigator's home.

4. IP addresses were not obtained from contributors' responses.

5. The principal researcher was the only one accessing the data.

6. Any materials were kept according to the IRB transcriptions coding sheet and stored in a locked box in the researcher's home for 3 years.

7. After 3 years, the researcher will shred all printed papers that were collected from participants and completely delete all electronic files.

Minimizing Risks

The potential risk of participation is designed to preclude any potential harm or breach of confidentiality. Participants in this research will be associated with no more than minimal risks. Minimal risk as described in the GPS IRB manual is that the design of the research should minimize all risks as much as possible, and any remaining risks should be clearly identified to the participants. Risks will be minimized in the following ways:

1. Participant's identity will not be revealed in the study and to the investigator.

2. Organizations name from participants will not be requested.

3. No personal information will be used or reported.

4. If the participant experiences any tiredness or irritability while contributing the survey, he or she can discontinue participation in the study.

Participants were clearly aware that their contribution to the study is fully voluntary. The participants had the choice to stop contributing in the survey at any moment without penalty. All participants signed a consent release form before the study, which explains that contributors can retract from the study at anytime, understand the input is voluntary, and agree to the confidentiality measure (see Appendix D). In addition, participants were capable to appraise the fallouts of the study for accuracy after it has been published on Pepperdine's dissertation database. Finally, participants were cognizant of their rights and provided with the Dissertation Chairperson Dr. Ronald Stephens' contact information: rstephen@pepperdine.edu along with the IRB Chairperson Dr. Thema Bryant-Davis' contact information: tbraynt@pepperdine.edu.

Confidentiality

Once participants coincide to contribute in the study, their identities and inputs will be kept confidential. The primary researcher will implement the following procedures to ensure confidentiality: (a) no names of participants will be requested from the study's survey, and participants will be identified as entrepreneur 1, 2, etc.; (b) all documents will be stored securely at the principal researcher's home; (c) quantitative data and electronic statistical will be saved in an external hard-drive with password protected; (d) IP addresses will not be connected to contributors' answers; and (e) all documents and electronic files will be destroyed after 3 years.

The principal researcher will file an application for a research exempt with the IRB as well as

file an application for waiver. The contributors will be cognizant of data-collection tools such as

online surveys questionnaires.

Definition of Data Gathering Approach

This research used a quantitative research methodology to collect data through an online

survey. According to Cammann (1980), the use of quantitative questionnaires in the form of

surveys is very useful of collecting data from participants. These data can be respondent's

opinions, ideas, imagination, and regional information. The use of quantitative method in

comparison of qualitative has certain benefits such as the data collected can simply be reported

and it can be easily recapitulated as well as analyzed. However, the use of qualitative method to

analyze data would be deep and detailed (Holton, 2005).

According to Pinsonneault and Kraemer (1993), demonstrated that "survey research has

three distinct characteristics. First, the purpose of the survey is to produce quantitative

descriptions of some aspects of the studied population. Second, the main approach used to collect

data is to ask people structured and predefined questions. Third, researchers typically collect data

about a fraction of the study population in such a way as to be able to generalize the findings to

the population" (p. 6). Therefore, survey research may be the most applicable method if the

investigator needs information that is not available elsewhere and wants to simplify the outcomes

to a larger population.

Data Analysis and Data Reduction

The analysis of quantitative data was attained through the methods of data reductions and data display. The collection and analysis of data promote new deliberations, learning, and additional positive change. The data were analyzed using quantitative content analysis, which helps transform observations of found categories into quantitative statistical data.

The following steps content analysis utilized Sato's (2007) in order to help transform observations of the collected data:

1. Listened to the taped interview while simultaneously reading the transcript as soon as possible to preserve currency of the experience and verify the accuracy (Burns & Groves, 2001; Norwood, 2000).

2. Identified themes by seeking recurrent responses while recognizing that variations are expected (Flick, 2002).

3. Correlated the highlighted areas and notes to the research questions (Norwood, 2000).

4. Tabulated the responses to determine frequency of occurrence (Burns & Groves, 2001).

5. Investigated the theme to determine the degree of integration to provide a description of the phenomenon studied (Speziale & Carpenter, 2007).

6. Used a second rater to provide inter-rater reliability through independent interpretation and analysis of the responses (Norwood, 2000).

Investigators measure and analyze the presence, values, and connections of such words and concepts, then make implications about the messages within the manuscript (Weber, 1990). The researcher decided what data to retain and what data to eliminate. Within this procedure, the data were organized into two cases: record retention and record discarding. According to

Sokolowski (2000), the main reason of phenomenology is to classify language into methods of

presentation that explains what the respondent is honestly saying, and to translate syntax into

meaning. Responses will be organized and themes will be classified per frequent responses.

Data Gathering Instruments

A research instrument is used to collect or measure data, which is related to an area under

the study. Questionnaires were conducted as a method of research instrument that addressed

queries to both novice and experienced entrepreneurs. The most applicable method of addressing

questionnaire to entrepreneurs is through a survey, which was considered into face-to-face and

telephone interviews. Through this process, the investigator elaborated the subsequent discussion

from the respondent's inputs. The current research instrument was conducting an online survey

to administer the questionnaires.

The objective of the survey is to gather adequate inputs to the five research questions: (a)

What are the essential core practices, strategies, and qualities that foster entrepreneurial success?

(b) What are the most important successful entrepreneurial qualities to embrace in a highly

competitive world market? (c) What factors are likely to result in a successful business? (d)

What core traits are essential to emphasize in a cyclical or uncertain market? and (e) What kind

of person makes a successful entrepreneur? A questionnaire is an applicable method for simply

gathering the data.

According to Annum (2014), questionnaire is a data gathering "instrument mostly used in

normative surveys. This is a systematically prepared from or document with a set of questions

deliberately designed to elicit responses from respondents or research informants for the purpose of collecting data or information" (p. 88). He also indicated questionnaire is a process of investigation document, which contains thoroughly complied and well structured series of inquiries intended to obtain the data. This provided insight to the study that investigates problems.

Data Gathering Procedures

Participants conducted an online survey that contains a list of questionnaires. A letter of confirmation was sent to their emails regarding the online survey. When the email was confirmed, a summary of the study was sent for each entrepreneur to review before conducting to the survey.

The survey method through Internet was appropriate and accessible to all participants, which allowed them to respond to the questionnaires at their convenient time. The participants were also acknowledged that their identities will be maintained confidential and anonymous. This would help participants to provide candid responses, minimize risks, and maintain motivation to contribute to the study.

Validity of Data Gathering Instruments

According to Cook and Campbell (1979), define validity as the "best available approximation to the truth or falsity of a given interference, proposition or conclusion" (p. 13). The concepts of validity are honesty, truth-value, sincerity, stability, transferability, and dependability of results. Wainer and Braun (1988) explain:

The validity in quantitative research as construct validity. The construct is the initial concept, notion, question, or hypothesis that determines which data is to be gathered and how it is to be gathered. They also assert that quantitative researchers actively cause or affect the interplay between construct and data in order to validate their investigation. (p. 181)

To attempt to confirm valid and reliable results, the current inquiry used the following recommendations by Morse (2002):

1. The literature review is used to inquire as to what known of the topic and to frame the research question; and the question will be revisited and modified if necessary.

2. Pre-test of interview topics and questions with a validity board of experts knowledgeable in the field to ensure appropriateness, and sensitivity to the data collected will maximized the chances of answering the research question. (p. 150)

According to de Vaus (2001), internal validity is the extent that the design of the research allows explicit conclusions can be conveyed from the results. The investigator is accountable for the validity in the data gathering. de Vaus suggests that investigators employ definite procedures to ensure internal validity and confirmation that the results avoid vague outcomes. Investigators in quantitative research should be always involved in the field of study and convey appropriate levels of knowledge to comprehend the context of the responses. The researcher for this study confirmed the outcomes of quantitative research, which was taken back to informants to act as member examining the truthfulness and sincerity of the interpretations. Academic colleagues will be debriefed regularly as to the outcomes, as part peer review. Finally, explanations of the findings will be systematic to determine transferability to other research (Creswell, 1998; de Vaus, 2001).

Reliability of Data Gathering Instruments

Reliability is perceived as the repeatability of the study. By writing a comprehensive explanation of the study procedure, higher reliability would be accomplished (Bryman & Bell, 2007). Stebbins (2001) indicated that reliability of a study would be valid when the research is collated and related with other research on the same topic. The present research maintained reliability as many scholars advise its goal. Reliability of the instrument was measured through a pilot study. A panel of three potential individuals was used to examine the survey and report for any ambiguous questionnaires they observe. Suggestions from this panel was reviewed by the researcher and created changes for any issues.

Summary

This chapter is designed to address the research questions and determined quantitative research methodology for this study. The characteristics of the research and participants are hereby proposed, as well as the methods of data gathering and analysis. The study used an online survey to collect the responses. A total of 15 entrepreneurs were sought to participate in this study. In addition, this chapter explains how the survey instrument would be designed to enhance the validity and reliability of data gathering process. Various topics, such as confidentiality, minimizing risks, and security of the data have been underscored as part of the key planning strategies to be embraced its this study.

Chapter 4: Results

Introduction

The purpose of this study was to identify key influential success factors for entrepreneurs to sustain a successful business. Fifteen entrepreneurs were surveyed via an online survey to identify factors affecting their business and to identify the necessary skills as a successful leader and entrepreneur. In this chapter, the researcher will present the findings of the analysis that was performed on the collected data. Participants in this study volunteered to contribute to the e-survey questionnaire and their identities are anonymous.

Table 5 displays the frequency counts for selected demographic variables. The age of the participants ranged from: 25-34 (33%), 35-44 (27%), 45-54 (20%), and 55-65 (20%). It was important to include participants of different ages in this study who may have different opinions based on their business ownership duration.

Table 5

Descriptive Statistics for Age Group

Age group:

#	Answer		Response	%
1	25-34		5	33%
2	35-44		4	27%
3	45-54		3	20%
4	55-65		3	20%
5	Over 65		0	0%
	Total		15	100%

(continued)

Statistic		Value
Min Value		1
Max Value		4
Mean		2.27
Variance		1.35
Standard Deviation		1.16
Total Responses		15

Table 6 displays the participants' highest level of education. Forty percent of the participants had a bachelor's degree, 33% had a master's degree, and 20% had a doctoral degree. There was only one participant who had an associate degree, which represent the last 7% of the group.

Table 6

Descriptive Statistics for Highest Level of Education

Highest level of education:

#	Answer		Response	%
1	Associate degree		1	7%
2	Bachelors		6	40%
3	Masters		5	33%
4	Doctorate		3	20%
	Total		15	100%

Statistic		Value
Min Value		1
Max Value		4
Mean		2.67
Variance		0.81
Standard Deviation		0.90
Total Responses		15

Table 7 displays the timeframe for the participants' years in business. The experienced entrepreneurs in this study represent: 8 out of 15 participants had their business for over ten years, 3 participants had their business for 5-10 years, and 2 participants had their business between 2-5 years. There were two novice entrepreneurs who had their business between 1-2 years. It was significant to include novice and experienced entrepreneurs in this study in order to analyze and share their success factors as a beginner and expert.

Table 7

Descriptive Statistics for Business Ownership Duration

Years in business:

#	Answer		Response	%
1	1-2 years		2	13%
2	2-5 years		2	13%
3	5-10 years		3	20%
4	Over 10 years		8	53%
	Total		15	100%

Statistic	Value
Min Value	1
Max Value	4
Mean	3.13
Variance	1.27
Standard Deviation	1.13
Total Responses	15

Table 8 displays the marital status of participants. Seven participants selected married, six participants are single, and only two participants are divorced/widowed. It seems from these statistics that the majority of participants are married, which could be a factor for the level of support. More statistics about the level of support will be detailed in Table 11.

Table 8

Descriptive Statistics for Martial Status

Marital status:

#	Answer		Response	%
1	Single		6	40%
2	Married		7	47%
3	Divorced / Widowed		2	13%
	Total		15	100%

Statistic	Value
Min Value	1
Max Value	3
Mean	1.73
Variance	0.50
Standard Deviation	0.70
Total Responses	15

Table 9 displays close-ended questions about participants' business and social experience. Approximately 67% of participants agreed that obtaining an academic degree was an important factor to start their business. However, only 33% participants selected "No." The next close-ended question asked, if entrepreneurs can benefit society? All participants concurred that entrepreneurs can benefit society.

Table 9

Descriptive Statistics about Business & Social Experience

Was obtaining an academic degree an important factor to start your business?

#	Answer		Response	%
1	Yes		10	67%
2	No		5	33%
	Total		15	100%

(continued)

Statistic		Value
Min Value		1
Max Value		2
Mean		1.33
Variance		0.24
Standard Deviation		0.49
Total Responses		15

Can entrepreneurs benefit society?

#	Answer		Response	%
1	Yes		15	100%
2	No		0	0%
	Total		15	100%

Statistic		Value
Min Value		1
Max Value		1
Mean		1.00
Variance		0.00
Standard Deviation		0.00
Total Responses		15

Table 10 displays a Likert response scale about participants' overall experience. The ratings were based on a 5-point scale: 1=Strongly Disagree, 2=Agree, 3=Neither Disagree or Agree, 4=Agree, and 5=Strongly Agree. Ten participants selected item 5 strongly agree to work 50 hours or more per week regularly. The Mean in this statement makes 4.60 out of 5. More than half of participants agreed that their family would support their going into business ($M = 3.93$). All participants agreed to accept both financial and career risks when necessary ($M = 4.60$). In statement 4, it seems that participants enjoy controlling their work assignments and making decisions affecting their work ($M = 4.53$). The highest levels of agreement were found with the statement "I believe that I am primarily responsible for my successes and failures ($M = 4.73$). Nine participants indicated that one or both of their parents were entrepreneurs, four participants disagreed ($M = 3.67$).

Table 10
Descriptive Statistics for Overall Experience

Please rate your overall experience where

#	Question	1: Strongly Disagree	2: Disagree	3: Neither Disagree or Agree	4: Agree	5: Strongly Agree	Total Responses	Mean
1	1- I am willing to work 50 hours or more per week regularly	0	0	1	4	10	15	4.60
2	2- My family will support my going into business	1	0	4	4	6	15	3.93
3	3- I am willing to accept both financial and career risks when necessary	0	0	0	6	9	15	4.60
4	4- I enjoy controlling my own work assignments & making all decisions affecting my work	1	0	0	3	11	15	4.53
5	5- I believe that I am primarily responsible for my own successes and failures	0	0	1	2	12	15	4.73
6	6- One or both of my parents were entrepreneurs	2	2	2	2	7	15	3.67

(continued)

Statistic	1- I am willing to work 50 hours or more per week regularly	2- My family will support my going into business	3- I am willing to accept both financial and career risks when necessary	4- I enjoy controlling my own work assignments & making all decisions affecting my work	5- I believe that I am primarily responsible for my own successes and failures	6- One or both of my parents were entrepreneurs
Min Value	3	1	4	1	3	1
Max Value	5	5	5	5	5	5
Mean	4.60	3.93	4.60	4.53	4.73	3.67
Variance	0.40	1.35	0.26	1.12	0.35	2.38
Standard Deviation	0.63	1.16	0.51	1.06	0.59	1.54
Total Responses	15	15	15	15	15	15

Table 11 displays descriptive statistics for participants' level of support. The table used a Likert response scale. The highest rated level of support was the "customers" ($M = 4.33$). Parents and mentors were also influential factors for the level of support of participants ($M = 4.21$). The lowest rated level of support was "college alumni" ($M = 3.27$). Some participants did not agree "spouse" is an aspect to help their business.

Table 11

Descriptive Statistics for Level of Support

Please rate your level of support:

#	Question	1: Strongly Disagree	2: Disagree	3: Neither Disagree or Agree	4: Agree	5: Strongly Agree	Total Responses	Mean
1	1- Spouse	0	2	8	1	4	15	3.47
2	2- Business partners	0	0	8	3	4	15	3.73
3	3- Customers	0	0	3	4	8	15	4.33
4	4- Mentors	0	0	3	5	6	14	4.21
5	5- Parents	0	1	2	4	7	14	4.21
6	6- Friends	0	2	2	4	7	15	4.07
7	7- Vendors	1	1	6	2	5	15	3.60
8	8- Acquaintances	0	2	6	3	4	15	3.60
9	9- Former co-worker/s	1	2	3	7	2	15	3.47
10	10- Friends of friends	1	1	5	5	2	14	3.43
11	11- Relatives	1	1	4	7	2	15	3.53
12	12- College alumnus	0	2	8	4	1	15	3.27

(continued)

Statistic	1-Spouse	2-Business partners	3-Customers	4-Mentors	5-Parents	6-Friends	7-Vendors	8-Acquaintances	9-Former co-worker/s	10-Friends of friends	11-Relatives	12-College alumnus
Min Value	2	3	3	3	2	2	1	2	1	1	1	2
Max Value	5	5	5	5	5	5	5	5	5	5	5	5
Mean	3.47	3.73	4.33	4.21	4.21	4.07	3.60	3.60	3.47	3.43	3.53	3.27
Variance	1.12	0.78	0.67	0.64	0.95	1.21	1.54	1.11	1.27	1.19	1.12	0.64
Standard Deviation	1.06	0.88	0.82	0.80	0.97	1.10	1.24	1.06	1.13	1.09	1.06	0.80
Total Responses	15	15	15	14	14	15	15	15	15	14	15	15

Table 12 displays descriptive statists for 14 elements of necessary leadership skills. These items were rated using a 5-point scale, where (1 = Strongly Disagree to 5 = Strongly Agree). Fifteen participants agreed that "integrity" and "ability to manage and motivate others" were the highest rated elements for necessary leadership skills ($M = 4.93$). The lowest rated elements were "political awareness" ($M = 4.00$), "make decisions quickly" ($M = 4.27$), and "transparent" ($M = 4.29$).

Table 12

Descriptive Statistics of Necessary Leadership Skills

Please rate your perceptions of necessary leadership skills:

#	Question	1: Strongly Disagree	2: Disagree	3: Neither Disagree or Agree	4: Agree	5: Strongly Agree	Total Responses	Mean
1	1- Honesty	0	0	1	2	12	15	4.73
2	2- Integrity	0	0	0	1	14	15	4.93
3	3- Has a purpose	0	0	0	2	13	15	4.87
4	4- Has respect to others	0	0	0	2	12	14	4.86
5	5- Vision to be successful	0	0	1	1	13	15	4.80
6	6- Ready to try new ideas	0	0	0	6	9	15	4.60
7	7- Ability to manage and motivate others	0	0	0	1	14	15	4.93
8	8- Intelligence	0	0	1	3	11	15	4.67
9	9- Transparent	0	0	3	4	7	14	4.29
10	10- Make decisions quickly	0	1	2	4	8	15	4.27
11	11- Self-confidence	0	0	0	3	11	14	4.79
12	12- Political awareness	0	0	5	4	5	14	4.00
13	13- Emotional intelligence	0	0	1	3	11	15	4.67
14	14- Diplomacy	0	0	2	3	10	15	4.53

(continued)

Statistic	1-Honesty	2-Integrity	3-Has a purpose	4-Has respect to others	5-Vision to be successful	6-Ready to try new wide ideas	7-Ability to manage and motivate others	8-Intelligence	9-Transparent	10-Make decisions quickly	11-Self-confidence	12-Political awareness	13-Emotional intelligence	14-Diplomacy
Min Value	3	4	4	4	3	4	4	3	3	2	4	3	3	3
Max Value	5	5	5	5	5	5	5	5	5	5	5	5	5	5
Mean	4.73	4.93	4.87	4.86	4.80	4.60	4.93	4.67	4.29	4.27	4.79	4.00	4.67	4.53
Variance	0.35	0.07	0.12	0.13	0.31	0.26	0.07	0.38	0.68	0.92	0.18	0.77	0.38	0.55
Standard Deviation	0.59	0.26	0.35	0.36	0.56	0.51	0.26	0.62	0.83	0.96	0.43	0.88	0.62	0.74
Total Responses	15	15	15	14	15	15	15	15	14	15	14	14	15	15

Analysis of Interview Question 1

How can you get potential investors to invest money in a start-up company? The average

participants agreed that entrepreneurs have to align their business with like-minded investors.

Out of the 15 participants, 8 indicated to come up with a viable and robust business plan and

show it to investors. It should include realistic financial forecasts that project revenues and expenses, a break-even point, and a rate of return. Out of the 15 participants, 5 suggested calculating how many shares an entrepreneur will distribute and at what stock price he/she would get this by valuing the company's book and market value. Then an entrepreneur would take a growth multiple and show many investors what his/her business is worth in future money. Depending on the capital structure, an entrepreneur would use Capital Asset Pricing Model (CAPM), or Weighted Average Cost of Capital (WACC) to calculate company valuation.

Only 1 of the 15 participants specified to start a company by seeding it by himself and involve family support as well as friends. The last participant recommended to start by contacting an accountant or private equity firms in your business area and asks if they might be willing to introduce you someone who could invest.

Analysis of Interview Question 2

How do you sustain a low cost of capital for a start-up company? Six participants suggested that an entrepreneur would decide if debt financing is logical or equity investing is better. Then an entrepreneur would be able to determine a lower to a higher cost of capital. However, when it comes to income statement, the goal is to obtain low operating expenses and high revenue. One respondent indicated that, "a low cost will result in very strong bottom line."

Out of the 15 participants, 5 indicated that initial capital expenditures could be minimized through outsourcing. Also, the efficient use of technology is an important and vital tool as well. The use of the cloud allows working from home offices as opposed to leasing office space. The other 4 participants recommended using Kickstarter or IndieGogo, which is pre-sales. They also indicated low-cost strategies might include leveraging receivables for cash similar to obtaining a cash advance on an entrepreneur secured revenues. Also, one effective way to sustain the low cost of capital is to negotiate sweat equity and/or performance compensation deals with professionals who have the 'know how' to obtain money fast and inexpensively. This can save money versus paying people in advance for capital-related services. Some participants advised that is never to pay any 'closer' or 'finder' money. Instead, make them perform first.

Analysis of Interview Question 3

What can a firm do to improve its cost of capital? Approximately 50% of the participants recommended that by working with experts in this area would improve the cost of capital. Each subsequent deal will be less expensive. For example, instead of having a single investor to invest $100,000, an entrepreneur can have ten investors to invest $10,000 each. Hence, an entrepreneur can access and negotiate with investors. It is easier to negotiate with smaller banks. Almost 35% of the participants advised eliminating debt. This will reduce the beta in the CAPM calculation. The cost of capital will determine the economic feasibility of a project to determine ultimately if the project is feasible or not. The goal is to have a low cost of capital and a high Net Present Value (NPV).

The last 15% of participants stated to invest in independent contractors, which should ideally create and organize workshops and training to improve human resources and hence maximize profits. Outsourcing increases the scale of production, and as the production costs become lower per unit of output, the firm has achieved economies of scale and thus improved its capital structure.

Analysis of Interview Question 4

How can you ensure competitive lead times? The majority of participants highly suggested watching and listening to what your competitors are saying at trade shows and speaking events. They often show and tell their latest products/services and reveal pieces of their future. Also by subscribing to their social media campaigns and other areas where they share information, can show their latest products and/or services. Hiring a research firm for the "lay of the land" and communicating with competitors' customers about products/services comparison. This would improve the business production by knowing the advantages and disadvantages of entrepreneurs' products/services. Having everything automated is critical – reports, communications, invoicing, delivery, returns.

An entrepreneur must continually re-evaluate market, and competitor trends and prices. Fast and efficient communication is imperative. Execution is also a key and important factor to implement or improve progress faster. If entrepreneurs failed to execute on the necessary steps, then someone that came second can still pass them. The last 20% of participants specified to have proper knowledge in Supply Chain Management, which consists of knowing the correct CRM software and purchasing software like SAP. In addition, an entrepreneur must not set the bar too high where companies cannot fulfill orders on time. Also, forecasting demand is critical to receive a good lead-time with customers.

Analysis of Interview Question 5

What would you say are the top 3 skills needed to be a successful entrepreneur? The top 3 skills were the following:

1. Quick and complete execution

2. Realistic/Accurate

3. Knowledge/Ingenuity

There were other essential skills listed by participants such as technical expertise, building relationships, judgment/decision making, unwavering leadership, initiative, flexibility, communication, motivation, stick-to-itiveness, setting expectations, perseverance, and taking risks. Only one participant listed "failing" as one of his skills needed to be a successful entrepreneur. He indicated if he had not failed a dozen times, he would not have the discipline, knowledge, and mindset to be an entrepreneur.

Analysis of Interview Question 6

How can you tell if there will be high demand for your product? The majority of participants indicated that an entrepreneur must begin with a thorough marketing analysis and examine industry trends. It takes research to find market segmentation; it takes some risk and patience. Some people want to create a product that might not be useful and start selling it, but do not have the patients to do the research. The other 3 participants signified that the quality of a product is critical and high demand is often a trick. It is far from the key ingredient to success. Profitability of a strong market product is key, as is ROI to investors. The way to know if your product is in high demand is when a customer (or reseller) will pay you for it, and then pays for it again. In other words, by making plenty of demos and trials with customers for valuable feedback.

Analysis of Interview Question 7

How can you build your reputation? Out of 15 participants, 13 recommended the following ways to build reputation:

- Social media channels (followers and sharing of info)

- TV Media

- Duns & Bradstreet

- BBB.org

- Newspaper

- Word of mouth

- The use of third-party validation tools such as PR

- Speaking events

- Testimonials from everyone including investors

- Paying bills on time

- Respond professionally to emails and phone calls on time

- Always give advance notice and offer alternatives if one cannot deliver on something

Two out of fifteen participants indicated that an entrepreneur builds a reputation through quality work and service, along with very strong customer service. In addition, integrity and honesty are foremost. One should under promise and over deliver.

Analysis of Interview Question 8

How can you prevent mistakes or damage control? Almost 50% of the participants indicated that one could not prevent mistakes. An entrepreneur must be very fast and thorough with damage control. This is why E&O and D&O insurance exists. Entrepreneurs can avoid mistakes by learning from them and making up for them with better performance as a result. Damage control is often made possible by a 'contingency' fund. Even if an entrepreneur can only allocate 1%, the 1% adds up over time. Plan for damage control – but do not over plan or make it a top priority. Severe damage control requires expert advisory and will be costly.

Nearly 30% of participants stated that mistakes could be prevented through learning from past experiences. An excellent quality control system should be set in place as well. As far as damage control, mistakes should be recognized and learned. Alternatives solutions need to be considered, and high value should be placed on customer satisfaction.

The last 20% of participants specified that believing in quality control is a priority. The standards of product quality must be top notch and always provide a feedback policy as well as a warranty protocol. By providing a warranty for a product or a service, forces the business owner to limit future issues.

Analysis of Interview Question 9

When should you seek venture funding? After analyzing the results from participants to this particular question, they shared different recommendations based on their investment experience. Some participants suggested avoiding investment until one could not continue in the business. One should seek venture funding when he/she has strong third-party validation. When an entrepreneur has his/her due diligence package complete and revenues are increasing, he/she should always go by referral – not cold.

Other participants indicated venture capital should be sought out when funds are needed to start, expand a business or to start or complete a project. Before funds are requested, a thorough financial projection and analysis should be created to determine the ability to repay the funds. Three participants preferred to seek venture funding when they want to expand their business and do not want to risk their personal money. In this case, they will ask for outside capital. The participants think the idea of sharing risk in a venture that could have future value is very noble.

Two out of fifteen participants would seek venture funding as soon as a viable business plan is in effect, and one can submit a substantial prospect. This process could take as little as a few weeks to several months depending on the market itself. Only one participant out of 15 suggested seeking funding between 3 to 5 years because at this stage a track record should be established.

Analysis of Interview Question 10

How can you get your first few clients? 7 out of 15 participants recommended by offering one service or product for free. One can go by referral to secure his/her first few clients. There is also no need to chase cold leads. One can get his/her first few clients by not placing his/her dreams on any particular client. It is the goal and not the role, meaning that if one client says 'no' then an entrepreneur finds another client until he/she receives the 'yes' because the 'yes' is what serves an entrepreneur overarching goal.

Out of 15 participants, 4 indicated that the first few clients could be acquired through trials and discounts. Those first few clients will be able to spread the word through word of mouth. Also, an aggressive marketing and advertising strategy is paramount. An online presence is also essential. The other 3 participants specified to receive their first few clients by establishing a robust lead generation pipeline online. Also, depending on the nature of someone's business, the strongest way to obtain customers is by giving them a no-risk trial period and see if the service meets their needs. Only 1 participant indicated to seek out individuals who are willing to take a chance on his business such as friends, family or new businesses. However, he stated establishing rapport is important. Also, some participants agreed to reach many companies/individuals as possible in order to acquire the first few clients.

Analysis of Interview Question 11

What motivates you? Approximately 35% of participants indicated that God is the first motivator because he put them the ability to control their destiny through knowledge. Thus, they are motivated by the word of God. It encourages their heart and keeps them on the right track. Some of these participants stated that there is something on the inside of them that keeps pushing them by working harder, smarter, stronger, and more efficiently.

Around 25% of participants stated aside from money, they think the fact that never being satisfied ever motivates them. Always creating a new vision and having goals and milestones to accomplish their vision is what drives them. What also helps the 25% participants is never to say the words "I can't"; instead, always saying the words "how can I?"

Nearly 20% of participants believed that helping people and fulfilling the needs of others seem to be a primary motivator for them. Almost 15% of the participants indicated that competition and success are what motivates them and, all in all, financial freedom, which must be achieved.

The last participant who represents the 5% specified that by working as fast as possible each day toward his weekly goals without rushing, his dream is coming true. He is also motivated because he has made up his mind that his success is inevitable – and not subject to circumstances – but subject to what he gives to his business, clients, and investors.

Chapter 5: Summary, Conclusions, and Recommendations

Introduction

This study was designed to identify the obstacles and benefits for building a start-up business and to identify the outcomes experienced by entrepreneurs. The results of this study showed that each entrepreneur had a different vision for establishing and maintaining a business. The experiences summarized in this study could be helpful to individuals who are planning to start a business. It is vital to be aware of the impact that difficult circumstances such as bad economic times, ineffective leadership, risky investment, and vigorous retaliation can have on the effectiveness of the business. Specific data and recommendations were provided to improve entrepreneurs' performance and maintain a successful business.

Summary of the Results

After an extensive analysis of the businesses studied in this research, it was apparent that entrepreneurs' plans are focused to accomplish their decision making in a well suitable manner and perspective way. Instead of directing people to concentrate on the obstacles that leaders could not find adequate methods to fix the business's issues.

It is apparent that entrepreneurs are taking less risk in uncertain economic environments because leadership control would be less effective inside the firm and through dealing with employees. Additionally, entrepreneurs would look for holes and gaps in their targeted market to determine whether they have a unique selling proposition that would fill the needs of the market. Managers are required to be experienced in identifying market trends and patterns so they can make educated decisions considering where to focus their effort.

The interviewees indicated that some organizations are presently financially stable even during the difficult economic times. However, research suggests that investing heavily during economic downturns is not recommended. If entrepreneurs need a good investment, they will gravitate toward products that are selling low at this time in order to be able to turn a profit in the future. Furthermore, by identifying what competitors are performing and who is succeeding and failing that would determine where and how entrepreneurs would invest their resources.

Entrepreneurs indicated that there were significant ways to obtain investors through leadership secrets such as face the reality, learn the culture, remove the boundaries, and be number one and keep redefining the market. Managers need to see a potential for return that justifies the risk of loss. They need to trust that individuals have the competence to succeed, or they need to be willing to take over for managers and be confident that they have the resources to achieve.

Entrepreneurs reported they faced multiple missions that jeopardized their success in order to achieve challenging tasks. One of the barriers listed was a lack of competence. It is clear that lack of leadership would be a reason to lead the company into failing. Directors must have the ability and leadership competencies such as effective written and verbal communication skills to facilitate the success of their business. Also, it is essential to assist employees in the development of their personal and professional skills.

In addition, all the interviewees concurred that leaders must have the power of verbal communication skills and making the image clear would spark employees' passion and efficiency. Furthermore, meetings require excellent communication, which will help the firm with the necessary revisions to make early changes in the plans in order to prevent possible problems, which will save time and money. In this case, the industry can identify the issues quickly and resolve them by discussing the strengths and weaknesses.

An important revelation in this study is that leaders considered are self-motivated, paid well, and receive good benefits, all of which contribute the productivity of each company. A company, which has incentives and bonus programs stimulates and creates momentum with employees to fulfill the company's vision.

Besides the reward program, entrepreneurs who anticipate and complete the necessary action plans, would increase production, and remain a world leader. Entrepreneurs can be influenced by their peers and develop ethical values in order to make decisions and exemplify these results towards the people around managers.

Recommendation of Instrument

The Social, Political, Economic, Legal, Intercultural, and Technical (SPELIT) model (Schmieder-Ramirez & Mallette, 2007) is an effective instrument to bring entrepreneurial success to an organization. The regional accrediting body mandates this plan, and this structure can help entrepreneurs evaluate their skills, identify their obstacles and risks when taking action, and provide successful business outcomes. This framework is also an efficient model when analyzing the current economic conditions and market share. This assessment can be viewed through the fundamental interactions of social, political, economic, legal, and intercultural knowledge.

Social Environmental Analysis

The key drivers for the social environment include awareness, relationships, and an over-riding service orientation. These key factors help entrepreneurs draw their attention to both the inner and outer work of leaders' qualities (Ashman & Zastrow, 2009). According to Schmieder-Ramirez & Mallette (2007), "Relationships are primary, everything else is derivative" (p. 37). Building relationships between organizations can result in a greater reputation and expanded market share. Relationships allow entrepreneurs to articulate an improved image of the organizational developments and strengths to external viewers. The third principal of social environment key drivers is service, which refers to the organizational purpose. It is imperative for entrepreneurs to be able to identify and solve any organizational issues. They must be adept at making decisions fairly quickly to serve the organization's needs. Most entrepreneurs are encouraged to ensure that they provide the best service in the community in order to prevent competitive lead times and grow profits.

Political Environmental Analysis

The political environment component is how an organization deals with benefits, views, assumptions, and standards. The purpose of the political module is to demonstrate how a leader can deal with organizational issues and apply political leadership skills to obstruct any critical problems. The SPELIT model can help a leader be knowledgeable and aware of politics and power to accomplish an organization's needs (Schmieder-Ramirez & Moodian, 2007). There are seemingly major problems that entrepreneurs face when dealing with political issues such as foreign policy laws. A foreign political matter could damage someone's business if he or she did not abide the country's law. Therefore, an entrepreneur needs to possess political knowledge and be aware of foreign policies in order to prevent possible or future interventions that can be problematic. The interpersonal perceptiveness and the ability to adjust one's performance are important factors for one's political skills to change stressful situations and gain control over the responses of the workforce.

Economic Environmental Analysis

A bad economy is a major issue for entrepreneurs where other foreign industries provide innovated products and services to the society. Therefore, an assessment of the economic conditions is critical to determine if an organization is capable to provide goods and services to the community. Entrepreneurship is an important factor to generate new jobs in the society and help prevent poverty in the community. According to Bednarzik (2000), entrepreneurship provides many opportunities for employment and improves economic situations. It leads people into a new society and achieves successful results such as a suitable reputation in the community as well as high profits. If entrepreneurs plan to launch a business with the purpose of gaining only money, then their possibility to sustain the business will quite likely not be satisfactory. Entrepreneurship is a procedure of generating something new and significant by dedicating the essential time and effort. Entrepreneurs are ambitious leaders who create a new environment with recruits and capital to produce new goods and services in the market.

Kemelgor (1985) pointed out that a few of the major reasons for failures of several entrepreneur's actions within the first three years included financial issues, lack of marketing skills, and lack of administration skills. He also suggested that entrepreneurs must make more effort to be trained in the administration practices in order to learn how to avoid the risks from competing entrepreneurial practices within the first three years.

Legal Environmental Analysis

Schmieder-Ramirez and Mallette (2007) posit that the legal element of the SPELIT is imperative because it helps leaders address what is codified in an organization. The process and policies of this legal element can help leaders to determine the internal culture and know how their decisions as legitimate leaders impact the internal and external atmosphere. The knowledge of legal policies and systems in the workplace is an important factor for one to become an effective leader. It is necessary to analyze and operate with different organizations by knowing the industry's legal system.

Intercultural Environmental Analysis

The meanings of culture, intercultural feeling, intercultural capability, and cultural intelligence must be established to create a successful environment. Culture is a method of mutual meanings consisting of actions, principles, and attitudes that expand within an organization and direct the behavior of its members (Morgan, 2006). Every culture has its own style of behavior and is clearly different from one country to another. Therefore, it is necessary for leaders to understand the importance of leadership behavior in diverse cultures in order to build corporations and market shares. Culture interventions through business have moral and immoral relationships, resulting in different consequences, such as a disagreement in an organizational environment.

An intercultural disagreement in the workplace is a common issue. Therefore, in order to make a successful corporate culture, leaders have to share values and behavior norms. Shared values are invisible, meaning that one has to infer them based on what people do and emphasize when they are talking. In contrast, behavior norms are agreed upon ways of behaving in an organization and evolve over time (Bailey, 1992). The norms are self-sustaining because people act in ways to support themselves whether or not they realize it.

In order to enhance corporate culture, entrepreneurs need to serve the consumer, worker, and clients' needs. Successful entrepreneurs design their entire industry system around customer loyalty. When entrepreneurs build connections with the society around them, then they will serve customers' needs in a better environment by understanding their culture. In addition, it is necessary for an organization to deliver superior value and win customer loyalty because market share and revenues increase the company's profits.

Literature Review Analysis

Organization improvement professionals consider that most problems and challenges are universal in nature. That is if entrepreneurs want an organization that rocks, they need to be aware that all the fundamentals of the system are aligned to rock (Haughton, 2004).

However, the biggest challenge for entrepreneurs was that they would not be able to guarantee employees' jobs during uncertain economic times because the company has to downsize before it is too late. According to Welch (2003), when downsizing primary appeared on the business landscape, it was taken as a sign of a severe decline in the downsizing company's fate or possibly worse as an avoidance of corporate social responsibility.

A successful entrepreneur certainly would apply leadership priorities in the workplace in order to create a thriving business. According to Welch (2003), "The art of leading comes down to one thing: facing reality and then acting decisively and quickly on that reality. In fact, business leaders who avoid reality are doomed to failure" (p. 8).

Characteristics of Successful Entrepreneurs

Regardless of one definition of success, there are an effective number of common characteristics that are shared by successful entrepreneurs. Even if one does not have all of these characteristics, he or she can be learned with practice and by developing a prosperous attitude. Stephenson (2009) shared some of theses characteristics:

1. Do what you enjoy: a personal satisfaction of enjoying practicing business leads to financial gains and stability. If someone does not enjoy what he or she is performing then, chances are a lack of success.

2. Take what you do seriously: Entrepreneurs cannot expect to be successful in business unless they believe in their products and/or services that they can sell.

3. Plan everything: the act of business planning is necessary because it involves research and analyzes of every business as well as makes conclusions based on the outcomes.

4. Manage money wisely: an entrepreneur needs cash flow to purchase inventory, pay for services, market his/her business, repair, and supply equipment. Therefore, "business owners must become wise money managers to ensure that the cash keeps flowing and the bills get paid" (p. 34).

5. It is all about customers: entrepreneurs' business is all about his/her customers, or clients. Therefore, an entrepreneur must be customer focused, including his/her policies, contracts, payment plans, and presentations.

6. Technology: Entrepreneurs should be keeping up with the high-tech world as it suits their needs.

7. Become an expert: an entrepreneur must have accurate information and expertise in his or her field.

8. Create a competitive advantage: a business should have unique selling proposition.

9. Invest in yourself: top entrepreneurs "read business and marketing books, magazines, reports, journals, newsletters, websites, and industry publications. They join business associations and clubs, and they network with other skilled business people" (p. 36). Also, they attend conferences, workshops, and training programs.

10. Be accessible: entrepreneurs must be cognizant and experienced about their products and services. They must provide clients with what they need and when they need it.

11. Build a good reputation: if an entrepreneur cannot provide the same level of products and services to clients, then entrepreneurs have no reason to trust their business, and without trust, an entrepreneur will not have a good reputation.

12. Sell benefits: sell the products and services by creating presentations, printing marketing materials, establishing a website, delivering newsletters, and attending events.

13. Get involved: by involving in the community to help local charity organizations or community events.

14. Master the art of negotiations: "the ability to negotiate effectively is unquestionably a skill that every business owner must make every effort to master" (p. 38).

15. Stay organized: an entrepreneur should develop systems for every business activity. Creating a calendar to manage tasks in order to ensure that tasks are all completed on schedule.

16. Follow-up constantly: by following-up with clients and business alliances is imperative. It enables an entrepreneur to increase sales and builds stronger business relationships.

Sutevski (2009) added additional critical key factors for entrepreneurial success. These factors are willingness to take action, creativity, patience, team player, risk taking, self-confidence, talent, and connections. It is possible that not every entrepreneur would possess all of the entrepreneurial successful factors and characteristics. However, combining some of the most important factors would make an entrepreneur build and manage a successful business. The table below by Frey (2013) shows the most significant characteristics of the 500 Fortune Companies:

Table 13.
Fortune 500 Companies Characteristics

Characteristic	Description
Vision	Fortune 500 companies have a clear vision stemming from top management as to what they are about and what they want to be. This vision is clearly communicated to all employees & used on a daily basis for making decisions
Empowerment	Employees are treated as though they are partners, not slaves, to the business. Employees are expected to constantly be learning new skills and growing, and the organization provides training and career development options to facilitate that growth.
Performance	Employee performance is measured and monitored in a way that encourages optimal performance. Goals are set for all major areas for performance, and feedback is routinely provided as to how employees are doing against those goals.
Profit	The company is profitable because being so is necessary to survive, but does not treat this objectives as its purpose for being. A company invests and involves in those transactions, which bring in profit for the company.
Team Approach	Employees are organized as much as possible into teams to facilitate the best

(continued)

Characteristic	Description
	means for solving problems, building morale, and creating synergy for achieving group and organizational goals.
Customer Service	Customers are treated as if they are the most important part of the business, which they are. Every employee and manager seeks to serve the customer or support those employees that are doing so. All work towards a common goal of customer satisfaction.
Quality	The company knows that long-term success depends in large part upon the long-term reputation of the company and so consistently seeks to develop lasting, quality relationships and to build quality products.
Communication	Management knows that communication is the oil that keeps the company operating smoothly. It seeks to communicate and to allow optimal opportunity for employees to communicate in any direction within the organization.
Ethics	The trustworthiness of a business, its customer service, its employee care, its way of dealing with customers and its urge to retain their old customers, is a part of the business ethics which plays an important role for long term success of companies.
Employee Management	An efficient reward system is present in these companies, to reward those who make steady improvements and perform beyond expectations, which includes profit sharing.

(continued)

Characteristic	Description
Acceptance to change	It requires the combined and managed efforts of many people in the organization over a period of one to three years.
Innovation	Companies generally focus in innovation in areas such as products or services development. It certainly helps them in maintaining their market leadership.

Note. Adapted from *Empowering the People* (p. 18), by J. K. Frey, 2013, Princeton, NJ: Princeton University Press. Copyright 2007 by First Princeton.

Should Entrepreneurs Act as a Leader or Manager?

The quality of a leader is not the same as the quality of a manager. According to Covey (2005), "leadership is not management. Management is a bottom line focus and leadership deals with the top line. Management is doing things right; leadership is doing the right things. Management is efficiency in climbing the ladder of success; leadership determines whether the ladder is leaning against the right wall" (p. 101). Leadership is mainly a high-powered, right intelligence activity. It is more of a talent; it is based on a philosophy.

Both the leader and manager are the producers and the problem solver. The manager administers, and the leader innovates. "Effective management is putting first things first. While leadership decides what first things are, it is management that puts them first, day-by-day, moment-by-moment. Management is discipline, carrying it out" (Covey, 2005, p. 148). Powerful entrepreneurs are leaders that regularly monitor environmental change and deliver the force needed to reform resources in the right path.

Leadership and management are not in the same place, but they are necessarily linked.

The table below by Bennis (1989) shows the differences between a manager and leader

Table 14.

A List of Differences between a Manager and a Leader

The Manager	The Leader
Maintains	Develops
Is a copy	Is an original
Focuses on systems and structure	Focuses on people
Relies on control	Inspires trust
Has a short-range view	Has a long-range perspectives
Asks how and when	Asks what and why
Has his/her eye always on the bottom line	Eye is on the horizon
Imitates	Originates
Accepts the status quo	Challenges it
Is the classic good solider	Is his/her own person
Does things right	Does the right thing

Note. Adapted from *On becoming a leader* (p. 51), by W. G. Bennis, 1989, New York, NY:

Addison-Wesley. Copyright 2009 by Basic Books.

DiSC Assessment

The need for DiSC assessment is a significant tool for many individuals. It helps discover the strength and weaknesses of leaders. DiSC stands for dominance, influence, steadiness, and conscientiousness, which is a personal assessment tool used by over a million people annually to improve work production, collaboration, and communication. It also helps deliberate leaders behavioral differences in organizations and social lie. Through this assessment, an individual will be asked to complete a series of queries about his/her behavior that produce a comprehensive report on his/her personality and performance. The DiSC questions are based on a rating scale (strongly agree, agree, neutral, disagree, strongly disagree) and there are no right or wrong answers. DiSC profile helps a leader to:

- Increase his/her self-knowledge about responding to disagreements, increasing motivation, and resolving problems that cause stress
- Facilitate better collaboration and lessen team disagreement
- Improving sales by discovering the style of a customer and responding to his/her needs
- Manage more successfully by understanding the personalities and priorities of colleagues and team members
- Become more self-conversant and active leader

Figure 9 below explains what DiSC stands for and what the letters mean.

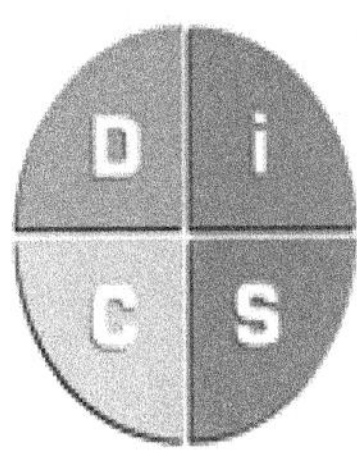

Dominance

Person places emphasis on accomplishing results, the bottom line, confidence

Behaviors
- Sees the big picture
- Can be blunt
- Accepts challenges
- Gets straight to the point

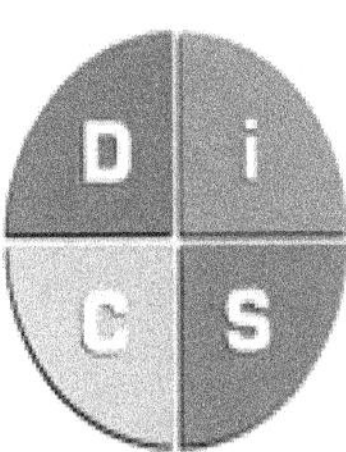

Influence

Person places emphasis on influencing or persuading others, openness, relationships

Behaviors
- Shows enthusiasm
- Is optimistic
- Likes to collaborate
- Dislikes being ignored

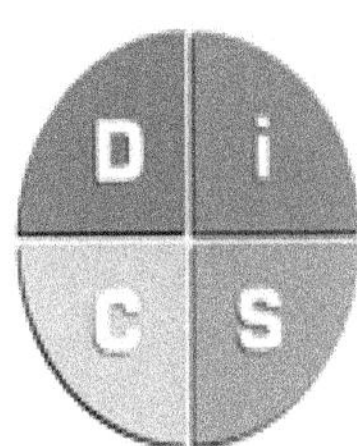

Steadiness

Person places emphasis on cooperation, sincerity, dependability

Behaviors
- Doesn't like to be rushed
- Calm manner
- Calm approach
- Supportive actions
- Humility

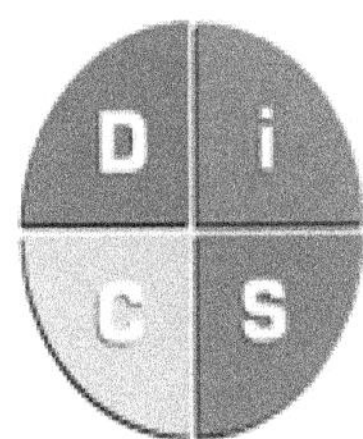

Conscientiousness

Person places emphasis on quality and accuracy, expertise, competency

Behaviors
- Enjoys independence
- Objective reasoning
- Wants the details
- Fears being wrong

Figure 9. What does DiSC stand for? What do the letters mean? Reprinted from *DiSC Personal Assessment*, In DiSC, n.d., Retrieved from http://discprofile.com/what-is-disc/overview. Copyright 1997 by DiSC Profile.

The challenge of DiSC assessment is to develop entrepreneurs' talents and make them more useful.

Leaders have the power to choose alternatives ways of thinking, acting, and behaving in the leadership activities for which they are responsible. These tools provide leaders with personal insights, a model to increase their flexibility in leadership behaviors, and resources to which they can return as they gain more experiences and become more multidimensional leaders. (DiSC, n.d., p 1)

Recommendations for Future Research

Today in the business world, it is important to stick to the facts and not digress. Entrepreneurs should have guidance to solve conflicts that might be problematic at their workplace. An effective entrepreneur has to be an expert at mollifying conflicts that can damage relationships and, therefore, have a negative impact on the business. The concrete steps that will be taken to improve entrepreneurs' ability and effectiveness in building a successful business would include:

- Administering the SPELIT model

- Taking the DiSC assessment

- Becoming an effective leader by applying leadership skills in the workplace

- Delivering superior work team

- Avoiding competitive lead times

- Improving cost of capital

- Collaborating effectively with local and global organizations

- Minimizing conflicts and disagreements

- Building a more positive reputation

Conclusion

The researcher selected 15 entrepreneurs from organizations that have been successful in growing the company's net worth. These entrepreneurs are the founder and CEO of their company and were invited to participate in this study. A survey approach was used to collect primary data. In addition, face-to-face and telephone interviews were conducted. Survey participants were sought from industries found through NASDAQ specializing in electronic devices, consulting services, educational programs, online services, and legal advice, among others. It was imperative to include various entrepreneurs who may have different visions and ideas of sustaining their business, which will facilitate the investigator to obtain multi ideas in order to maintain a successful business. This study shows major problems, which entrepreneurs must overcome to stay in business. The problems include lack of financial support, inability to understand foreign policies, intercultural disagreement, leadership skills, and competitive lead times. By using the SPELIT model, however, entrepreneurs will be able to understand and solve their major issues in many areas such as political, economic, legal, intercultural, and technical. The outcomes will facilitate entrepreneurs to overcome their barriers and articulate a successful organization. The results of this study shows that entrepreneurs are successful insofar as they maintain:

- Effective entrepreneurial skills to manage employees through leadership attributes such as confidence, self-awareness, emotional intelligence, diplomacy, training, and motivation.

- Ability to obtain financial support from investors, family, friends and/or government

- Overcome competitive lead times

- Provide ongoing training programs

- Cooperate with different organizations

- Understand different cultures

- Establish superior working teams

- Make quick and workable decisions making

- Powerful communication skills

- Energize others

- Build trust among employees

These traits are imperative for entrepreneurs to bring entrepreneurial success to their organization. In addition, motivation is a significant factor for entrepreneurs to inspire their employees and endure in business in the long-term. This study would help entrepreneurs and individuals to be able to identify and analyze their strengths and weaknesses and learn how to maintain and lead a successful organization.